THE 10% PROJECT®

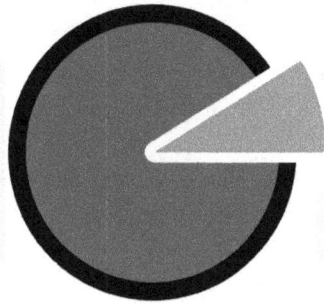

SMALL SIDE PROJECTS THAT TRANSFORM YOUR CAREER & LIFE

SUSAN RYAN

Roo
Goose
PRESS.

SYDNEY | SAN FRANCISCO

For permissions or inquiries, please contact:
RooGoose Press | www.10PercentProject.com

Library of Congress Control Number: 2025909595
ISBN: 979-8-9988904-0-6
Cover design by Susan Ryan
Book design by Susan Ryan
Printed in the United States of America

First edition, 2026

For my Gorgeous Husband —
my rock, my calm in the chaos,
and the one who keeps me laughing
every step of the way.

And for Gabby —
the dancer, the dreamer, full of love, joy,
and all the best surprises.
You light up every room and
remind me what magic looks like.

Praise for

THE 10%
PROJECT®

"The 10% Project made dreaming big feel easy
by starting small. Exactly the reminder I needed."

———————————

"Working on my 10% Project reignited my passion —
I finally feel excited about my career again."

———————————

"I always thought big changes needed big risks.
The 10% Project showed me a smarter,
braver way forward."

———————————

"Every workplace should teach this —
I finally feel like I own my career journey."

———————————

"Working on my 10% Project changed everything —
it gave me the courage to finally move forward."

———————————

"I had no idea one small project could
shift my career path this much.
Thank you!"

CONTENTS

A 10% Project in Your Hands

This book isn't just about 10% Projects — **It is one.**

A 10% Project is something you do for yourself.
Because **you** believe in something.
Because **you** feel a pull.
Because **you** know, deep down, that you can make a
difference — even in just one small, meaningful way.

The fact that you are reading this now, holding the 10%
Project Book in your hands, is the best proof I can give you
that it works. This book is my 10% Project. I didn't have a big
budget. I didn't have a publisher, a designer, a marketing
machine, or a team of editors. I had a full-time job. A young
daughter. A messy, beautiful, real life. And I had an idea I
couldn't let go of.

I wrote it the same way many of you will pursue your own
ideas — fueled by belief, stubborn hope, and the support of
my family, friends, and community. It was created on
weekends, in early mornings, late nights, during my
daughter's ballet lessons, and in the midst of life's beautiful
chaos. No permission from anyone else. Just belief, passion,
a laptop, and a whole lot of stubborn hope.

It wasn't easy. But it mattered — to me.

And here's what I've learned:
When we give even 10% of our time to something that lights
us up — something that feels like **ours** — we come alive.
Braver. Clearer. Kinder. More fulfilled. And yes — happier.

If something in these pages helps you, even just a little...
pass it on. Tell someone. Share it. Or leave a message for me
at _www.10PercentProject.com_.

You never know who might need to hear it.
That's how 10% Projects work:
One small, bold step at a time — shared forward.

"The best way
to predict the future
is to create it."

Peter Drucker

SECTION 1
Introduction

Setting the Stage for Change

Welcome! I'm so glad you're here.

You're not just reading a book. You're standing at the starting line of a whole new kind of journey — one that doesn't demand you flip your life upside down, but instead invites you to take one small, bold step at a time.

The 10% Project isn't about massive life overhauls or intimidating leaps. It's about carving out a small space — just 10% of your time — and daring to invest it in something that stretches you. Something different. Something exciting. Something that, over time, could change absolutely everything.

Because here's the key:

If you invest 10% of your time in a 10% Project — inside or outside of work — it can completely change 100% of your life.

When you give 10% to something that lights you up, it doesn't just change that project — it changes how you show up in the other 90%. I've felt this shift myself, and I've seen it in others. The energy spills over — into your mood, your mindset, your relationships. That's the real magic.

Tiny, intentional steps, that compound over time, creating momentum, shifting opportunities, and reshaping what you thought was possible.

Over the years, I've found that real growth doesn't come from waiting for permission or chasing massive overnight transformations. It comes from small, intentional actions. A curious spark. A simple "what if?" A choice to follow a flicker of energy instead of ignoring it.

That's the magic of a 10% Project: no waiting around for permission to begin. It teaches you to trust that tiny shifts — pursued consistently — create big opportunities.

The reality that no one tells you: degrees, credentials, and resumes are helpful — I have a few myself — but they're not enough. What really opens doors, what changes perceptions, what creates momentum, are the small, consistent ways you show the world who you are, and who you are *becoming.*

Behind every "lucky break" I've experienced was a 10% Project that built new skills, expanded my network, and prepared me for opportunities I didn't even know were coming. No magic. No shortcuts. Just small, joyful, intentional steps.

You don't have to be the loudest, the boldest, or the most connected person in the room. You just need to be brave enough to start. To claim your 10% space. To let it take you somewhere new and rewarding.

This book is your invitation. It's a roadmap for anyone who's tired of waiting, stuck wondering, or ready for more. You'll find tools to help you ignite your spark, map your first steps, navigate the inevitable twists, and celebrate every small victory along the way. You'll see that it's not about overhauling your life — it's about adding something meaningful and new to it.

You don't need anything more than this book to kick off your own 10% Project - However, sometimes a little extra motivation or structure can help... if that's you, check out the Appendix of this book for more resources or visit: www.10percentproject.com.

Because every big dream starts small. Every big leap begins with a simple hop.

Let's chart your course. Let's find your 10%.
Let's start small. Dream big. Make it happen.

Before we go any further...

You're about to enter the heart of the 10% Project — the foundation explaining why the 10% Project concept works.

These next chapters lay the foundation:

- What is a 10% Project.
- Why it works for absolutely anyone.
- The psychology that makes small steps powerful.
- How tiny actions, or hops, turn into real-life momentum.

Reading the content in order is the path I recommend — the "standard" route.

If you're the kind of person who likes to *jump in* (I see you!), feel free to hop straight to **Section 3** to start your 10% Project today.

But when you have a moment, come back here.

These early chapters give you the fuel — the spark, the psychology, the "why it works" — that will make your project deeper, easier, and more sustainable.

That said....

Start now.
Start later.
Just start!

Small Steps. Big Shifts
The Global Roots of the 10% Project

We all love stories of sudden transformation — the overnight success, the dramatic pivot, the big leap. But if you zoom out across history, the real game-changers usually didn't start big. They started small — with quiet, consistent steps that gained power over time.

That's the magic of a 10% Project.

And it's not a modern invention. It's a timeless truth that shows up again and again: **a small, focused effort, offered regularly, can lead to life-altering impact.**

In The Beginning

Across ancient cultures, a tenth was sacred. A portion of your harvest, your income, your time — set aside for something greater.

In Judaism — one of the world's oldest *and still thriving* monotheistic traditions — the practice of **ma'aser** (tithing a tenth) dates back more than **3,000 years**, woven into agricultural life and spiritual responsibility.

Whether it was **tithing** in Christian traditions, **dāna** in Buddhist and Hindu cultures, or **zakat** in Islam, the idea was the same: you gave to honor your role in something bigger than you.

It was community. Contribution. Alignment. It was about intention.

The Bridge: The 10% Project

That's what the 10% Project is: a reimagined ritual. It's not about religious obligation or abstract self-help. It's about carving out 10% of your energy, time, or attention for something *that lights you up* — and usually, ends up serving others too.

It's how we honor a timeless human impulse — to give, to grow, to reach upward — in a way that fits modern life.

A New Offering for a New Era

Today, giving 10% of your income isn't always possible. But giving 10% of your *ideas*? Your time? Your courage? That's not just possible. It's powerful.

When you give to your own development, you multiply what you can offer to others. When you grow, it impacts everything you touch, and the people around you grow too.

The ancient tithe helped us survive together. The modern 10% Project helps us evolve together.

The Butterfly Effect: You Never Know What Might Happen

There's a concept in chaos theory called the *butterfly effect.* The idea that a butterfly flapping its wings in one part of the world could set off a tornado somewhere else.

It's a poetic way of explaining **sensitive dependence on small events** — how one tiny action, unnoticed at the time, can ripple into massive consequences.

That's what your 10% Project can become.

A side project that sparks a new career.
A single blog post that gets shared with the right person.

An email, a phone call, a prototype, a workshop — small on the surface, but powerful in the way it changes how you think, grow, and connect.

You don't have to predict the outcome. You just have to start.

Why 10% Works

It's **manageable** — just enough to matter, never so much that it overwhelms.

- It's **visible** — people remember consistent momentum more than a one-off dramatic flair.
- It's **personal** — no two people use their 10% the same way.
- And most of all, it's **empowering** — you're not waiting for change. **You're creating it.**

Throughout history, 10% has consistently reappeared. Not because it's the "perfect" amount — but because it's a *doable* amount.

A tenth is enough to build something new without tearing everything down. It's a rhythm. A pulse. A step forward — again and again — until suddenly, you're standing somewhere completely different than where you began.

Just start...

The 10% Project is part of a lineage — a long, quiet legacy of small steps leading to big shifts. You're not just doing a side project. You're joining a tradition of people who believed that **you don't have to give it all to make a difference** — you just have to start somewhere.

So, start with 10%.
Not as a rule, but as a rhythm.
Not to impress anyone, but to align with yourself.
Not to overhaul your life, but to shape it —
one small, bold step at a time

"What road do I take?"
"Well, where are you going?"
"I don't know."
"Then it doesn't matter.
If you don't know where you're
going, any road will take you
there."

Alice in Wonderland
& The Cheshire Cat

SECTION 2
The 10% Project

CHAPTER 1

10% Projects Change Your Life

You've already taken the first step by opening this book.

Now, let's dive deeper into the 10% Project concept — and why it could be the most life-changing 10% you ever invest in yourself.

This is more than just an idea—it's a strategy anyone can use to create new opportunities, learn fresh skills, make powerful new connections, expand their network, and gain a real sense of accomplishment.

A 10% Project is a small but deliberate effort, regularly carving a little time out to upgrade your life or career. It doesn't require blowing up your routine—it's about weaving meaningful, manageable changes into your day-to-day life.

One of the core principles? Pick something that genuinely lights you up. Maybe it's learning a new skill, deepening relationships, diving into a passion project, or tackling a problem you've spotted at work or in your community. Your 10% Project is your launchpad for taking control and unlocking opportunity.

Most successful people already do this—often without even realizing it. Whether you've unintentionally dabbled in 10% Projects, or never even heard of the concept before now, this book is your step-by-step guide to discovering and designing your own 10% Project.

If you've ever felt stuck, like your potential is quietly collecting dust—or you're ready to steer your life with more intention but aren't sure how—then starting with a 10% Project might be the best move you make all year.

The world is packed with smart, capable people doing great work—and if you're holding this book, chances are you're one of them. And yet, again and again, we see talented people overlooked, passed by for promotions, or boxed into roles that don't showcase their full potential.

It's frustrating—and honestly, it doesn't always make sense. Even worse, it can leave even the most driven people demoralized, watching opportunities go to others while their own growth stalls.

So why is it that some people—no more talented than you— seem to land all the opportunities and rise through the ranks, while others, just as hardworking and capable, stay invisible?

If you're one of those talented people watching others (maybe with less potential) get the spotlight while you're stuck waiting your turn—you know just how confusing, even maddening, that can feel.

You're exactly who I had in mind when writing this book. But really, anyone, in any life stage or any situation, can use 10% Projects to spark opportunity.

Whether you're employed, unemployed, retired, a student, or somewhere in between—the core principles behind 10% Projects apply. They open doors. They create momentum. They work. I guarantee it.

Where It All Began

For years, I've had the privilege of speaking to classes of MBA students from The Ohio State University who visit Silicon Valley as a part of their program. Honestly, I'm thrilled they keep inviting me back — there are plenty of bigger names they could hear from. Maybe it's because my story isn't shiny.

It's messy. Real. From massive global corporations to scrappy, chaotic startups — and somehow making it all work.

As I mentioned in the introduction, when I looked back across my career, I realized that almost every "lucky break" I've experienced was a direct result of a 10% Project that built new skills, expanded my network, and prepared me for opportunities I didn't know were coming. That realization was so meaningful to me, that I created a slide showing the key 10% Projects that changed my life (that chart appears in the following pages).

I shared this with the MBA students – encouraging them to always have a 10% Project underway because of their ability to help you continuously learn, and for the many opportunities they unlock.

Thinking back, I realized how often the energy in the room shifted when I shared the concept of the 10% Project. Every time, I could see 'lightbulbs' go on in the audience, I saw the students noting down the ideas I shared about using 10% of their available time to invest in learning something new, and how it could open doors for them throughout their entire career.

After one presentation, when I shared the concept of the 10% Project, an amazing MBA student, Liz, came up to me. She said, "I love your marketing stories, but you have to write a book about the 10% Project. That's what I'm going to remember." And the students around her nodded in agreement.

As I thought more about the idea of a 10% Project Book, and floated my ideas past some of my friends, it turned out Liz was right – people were interested in hearing about the 10% Project and did feel it was a strategy that would help them in their career. **So the idea for this book was born.**

If you feel stuck, if you're craving more, if you're tired of waiting for someone else to give you a chance —
this is for you.

What if you carved out just a small slice of time for something that excites you? What if that tiny shift opened doors you had never imagined?

In this book, I'll help you find your own 10% Project — and show you how to make it count.

Because small, steady effort does change lives. And it doesn't take a total life upheaval.

It takes 10% of your time — invested in yourself — one small, bold step at a time.

Real Life... Real Talk...

Throughout this book, you'll see stories, lessons, and little side-door reflections I've gathered from years of personal and professional growth.

When you see the "Real Talk" icon, that's where I'll share the messy middle — the behind-the-scenes wins, the facepalm-worthy fails, and the lessons I learned along the way.

Think of them as coffee break moments — less polished, more personal, but always shared to help you feel a little less alone on your journey.

The following chart highlights many of the 10% Projects that led to major changes in my life, with the full stories explained in Chapter 32. And beyond those? There are even more ideas sitting quietly in my 10% Project file — half-started dreams and glimmers of possibilities just waiting for me.

Because dreaming doesn't stop. It just keeps evolving, one small bold step at a time.

The 10% Projects that Changed my Life

Undergraduate
Psychology

Public Relations &
Masters in Marketing

The Boeing
Leadership Center

MACQUARIE University
SYDNEY·AUSTRALIA

UTS
UNIVERSITY OF TECHNOLOGY, SYDNEY

1990's → 2000's

Sydney Australia

Melbourne Aust. | St Louis

Local Govt Agency Subsidiary

Municipal Library

Ad Agency
MARKETING STRATEGY

Air Traffic Control Software

10% PROJECT **Children's Activities** >PR Officer

10% PROJECT **Graphic Design** >Boeing Position

10% PROJECT **Seattle Conference** >Boeing Networking

Public Relations
LOVING LIVING
Ku-ring-gai Council   KU-RING-GAI

Corporate Travel

10% PROJECT **Off-Set Program** >Relocation to USA

10% PROJECT **Charity Fundraiser** >Marketing Position

Boeing Leadership Center

10% PROJECT **Networking** >Corporate Position

The 10% Projects that Changed my Life

Executive MBA
Northwestern University

Digital Marketing
& Social Media

Kellogg
School of Management

Berkeley
UNIVERSITY OF CALIFORNIA

2010's

Chicago | Seattle   United Kingdom | St Louis

Fortune 50 Corporation

Corporate HQ

International M&A

T-X

10% PROJECT **Boeing Team Building** >Kellogg MBA

10% PROJECT **Marketing Audit** > COS Role

Commercial Airplanes

Boeing Global Services

JSTARS

Space Shuttle

10% PROJECT **Marketing Training** > HX Connection

10% PROJECT **Venture Research** > HX Marketing

The 10% Projects that Changed my Life

Design Thinking & Product Management

Cornell University

Coaching | Training & Lecturing

STARTUP

2010's   2020's

Silicon Valley, California

Corporate VC   Start-ups

BOEING HORIZONX
Corporate Venture Capital

BOEINGNEXT
New Business Ventures

Personal Air Vehicles

Cargo Air Vehicles

10% PROJECT — Strategizer Training > Start-up Support

Portfolio Support

MATTERNET

FORTEM TECHNOLOGIES

sparkcognition

UP SKILL

NEAR EARTH AUTONOMY

RoboticSkies.

C360 A VIDEO REVOLUTION®

MORF3D

Unmanned Surface Vehicles

10% PROJECT — Ohio State
> 10% Project Book
> Start-up Mkting Book

10% PROJECT — Marketing Plan
> VP Position

Thermal Solutions

10% PROJECT — 10% Project Book
>Corporate Presentations

10% PROJECT — Start-up Mkting Book
>VC Sponsored Start-up Training

CHAPTER 2:

What Exactly is a 10% Project?

The idea behind a 10% Project is deceptively simple: it's something you take on outside your regular routine—something that is intentional, action-driven, and designed to spark change, solve a problem, or open a new opportunity.

Dedicate just 10% of your time to something that stretches you — something new, different, and energizing. Something that sparks joy, builds new skills, expands your network, and opens new doors.

When I first developed the concept of the 10% Project, I saw it as a powerful way to jumpstart your career—something that could help you stand out at work and fast-track growth by showcasing your initiative and drive.

But after hundreds of conversations with people from every walk of life—each with different goals, challenges, and dreams—I realized something bigger: 10% Projects aren't just for career advancement. They can benefit anyone, anywhere.

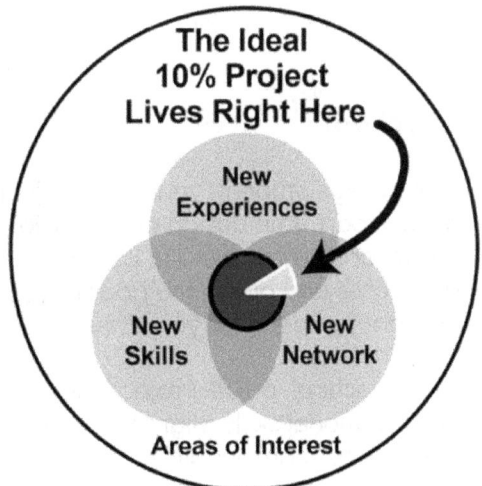

The Ideal 10% Project Lives Right Here

New Experiences

New Skills

New Network

Areas of Interest

Whether you're starting out, starting over, or somewhere in between—this concept meets you where you are. Let's break it down.

At Work

If you're currently employed, a 10% Project might involve spotting a smarter way to get things done, identifying an untapped opportunity, or launching a small initiative that drives impact—creating a plan to attract new customers, improving processes to increase efficiency, creating a new approach to sourcing to cut costs, or creating a new creative space to spark collaboration.

If You're Job Hunting

A 10% Project could be your secret weapon—building connections, learning in-demand skills, or creating a portfolio piece that helps you stand out and land that dream role.

At Home

Maybe it's finally writing that book, picking up a new activity, or launching a passion project you've always talked about, but never felt ready for. Your home life is fertile ground for meaningful 10% Projects.

At School

As a college student, your 10% Project could mean launching a small part time design business, joining (or starting) a cause, or learning a skill that sets you apart from other graduates and opens the door to your dream job. Think of it as planting seeds for your future.

In high school, a 10% Project showcasing leadership or organizational skills might be the key to impressing the admissions team, leading to acceptance into your dream college.

For Children

Kids aren't thinking about careers—yet. But they're forming the habits and attitudes that will define how they tackle life. This is where it begins. 10% Projects can give kids a way to plan, tinker, create, and follow through, giving them something priceless: confidence and a belief in their own abilities.

In Retirement

Just retired and wondering what's next? In retirement starting a 10% Project can keep you sharp, socially connected, and creatively engaged—without the pressure of a full-time commitment.

The ideas and opportunities are only limited by your imagination. If you're new to this concept, you might find some thought starters in the case studies section later in this book. Once you start thinking about possible 10% Projects, you'll begin to see that opportunities are everywhere, just waiting for someone to act.

The Two Big Ideas that make a 10% Project Effective

There are two big ideas that separate the 10% Project from the way you may have approached new ideas in the past...

10% Projects are always **_INTENTIONAL_** and **_TANGIBLE._**

Being Intentional

The concept of a 10% Project is simple—but life isn't. It's shockingly easy to drift through our days on autopilot, checking boxes instead of chasing purpose.

The people who stand out—the ones who grow fast and get noticed—are intentional. They invest their time in building skills, gaining experiences, and growing meaningful connections. Want to be one of them? It starts with how you use your time.

Choosing a 10% Project is making a promise to yourself. Pick something that aligns with your bigger goals or vision—something that energizes you, something that truly inspires you. Then you use every opportunity your 10% Project unlocks to build momentum and grow.

The real value of a 10% Project comes from the simple act of doing it—planning it, documenting it, and leveraging every bit of value it will create for you—because even the smallest steps can lead to big shifts.

Making it Tangible

So often I hear from people frustrated that their voice is not being heard - that their ideas are being overlooked. Following the concept of a 10% Project ensures your brilliant ideas are showcased in a way that demonstrates the value they could bring. The approach ensures that the people around you see the way you think, how proactive you are, and the skills you can bring to anything you're associated with.

Making your ideas tangible and then sharing them, ensures that they are heard and considered. It also ensures everyone who hears about the idea knows it came from you and therefore enables you to receive the maximum benefit from them.

Creating Opportunities

When people hear about 10% Projects, they often think, "Wait—I've done this kind of thing before." Maybe they took the initiative, shared an idea, or made something better. Often, those moments ended up unlocking something: a promotion, a new connection, a fresh skill, or simply recognition they'd been missing.

Others remember spotting problems or opportunities—but they didn't act, either because they were overwhelmed or distracted.

Some people did share their ideas, talking to colleagues... only to watch someone else run with them and reap the rewards. (*Oof.*)

The fix? Own your ideas. When you document, plan, and act with **intention**, when you make your ideas **tangible** you protect the value—and make sure it benefits *you.* Turn your ideas into 10% Projects, document them, own them. Doing this simple 10% Project step places your name up front and center on your idea... ensuring you get the credit for identifying the opportunity or problem, and proposing a solution.

To find your next 10% Project, look around: What's bugging you? What could be better? Where do your interests and frustrations intersect? Pick something that excites you—and plan your first step. That's it.

The power of the 10% Project is in treating your ideas like they matter—because they do. Make it a project. Take ownership. That's how you get real, lasting value.

And here's the best part: it's not hard. You can do this!

Case Study Snapshot: Turning a Bold Idea into a Career Leap

While working in Melbourne, Australia, at a subsidiary of The Boeing Company, I spotted a hidden opportunity: a need for investment tied to a major government sale. It wasn't part of my core role — but I decided to think about it anyway.

Through a self-initiated 10% Project, I researched the topic, built a case, documented it, and pitched the idea of using the international investment to create a defense-focused export product. Aligning multiple Boeing divisions, the U.S. Air Force, the Australian Air Force, and both the U.S. and Australian governments wasn't easy.

And while the major government sale itself was eventually paused, for me personally, my 10% Project changed everything.

My initiative, strategic thinking, and the network I built, caught leadership's attention — and directly led to a life-changing opportunity: relocating to the U.S. to teach leadership and marketing to emerging leaders and company executives at the Boeing Leadership Center in St Louis, Missouri.

Key Takeaway: *Even when a project doesn't "succeed" in the traditional sense, the skills, visibility, and relationships you build can open doors you never expected.*

You can read the full story in Chapter 32: "Offsetting Challenges: Turning a Bold Idea into a Leadership Leap."

7 Simple Steps to a 10% Project

Here's a simple, seven step framework to help you spark, shape, and supercharge your 10% Project.

Step 1: Ignite Your Spark
Reflect on your personal goals—what matters most to you right now?

Step 2: Find Your 10% Project
Spot a meaningful idea—something you can improve, create, or launch.

Step 3: Own It.
Write it down. Capture the what, why, and how. Give it a name!

Step 4: Chart the Course
Map out your plan in clear, doable steps. Small actions, real momentum.

Step 5: Share the Vision
Share it! Rally support or just tell someone. Accountability helps.

Step 6: Reflect and Refine
Gather feedback, reflect, and refine. Flexibility = growth.

Step 7: Jump Into Action
Take action. Start small... but start.

Don't worry—we'll dive deeper into each step in the next section. You'll have guidance every step of the way.

If your 10% Project is work-related, positioning is critical - making sure it's seen the right way by the right people. You also need to make sure you're perceived to be doing a really good job before launching a 10% Project. (We'll dig into exactly how to do that later in this book.)

If it's a personal project? Awesome—you're the boss. Prioritize it, protect your time, and give yourself permission to follow through.

What a 10% Project is NOT

- It's not hard to do.
- It doesn't cost anything.
- No special skills are needed—anyone can start today.
- You don't need a coach or consultant. Just you and your idea.

- No fancy courses or certifications are required.
- You don't need opportunity to "fall in your lap"—you create it!
- You don't need permission, connections, or a big team.
- It's entirely in your hands to start—and to benefit from.

IMPORTANT NOTE:

The Power of the "Third Really" Doing a really, really, really, great job.

Before you start thinking about 10% Projects, there's one thing you have to lock down...

Do your core job really, really well. *This holds true for anything that you are already committed to doing on an ongoing basis... whether your 'core job' is the position you currently hold at work, running your own business, or parenting your children.*

If you're already delivering great results — if you're the one people know they can count on, the one knocking it out of the park, you always get exceeds expectations on your reviews — congratulations. That's the foundation. That's what earns you the credibility to carve out space for more.

But here's the opportunity: Once you're already seen as a top performer, and you're already doing a really, really great job, what do you do with that **extra** *10% of your energy and time?*

You could spend it making your core job even more perfect — chasing a third "really". Doing a really, really, "really" great job.

Or... you could invest that third "really" into something unexpected.

Something that surprises people.

Something that opens doors people didn't know you were even ready for.

That's where the magic happens.

Your excellence buys you freedom.
Your 10% Project uses it.

Curious? Inspired? Fired up?

Let's go deeper into how you can turn your own 10% Project into action—***starting now!***

CHAPTER 3:

The 10% Project & Psychology

Before we jump into the framework, it helps to understand the psychology behind why 10% Projects work so well. This chapter explores two powerful motivation theories — Maslow's Hierarchy of Needs and Self-Determination Theory — and shows how the 10% Project naturally activates both.

Maslow, Self-Determination Theory, and Why Small Steps Spark Big Growth

Most of us have our basic needs met.
We have food, safety, a place to sleep, people we care about.

And yet...
Sometimes we still feel stuck.

Psychologist Abraham Maslow believed there was a reason for that.

Maslow's Hierarchy of Needs — and Why It Still Matters

In the 1940s and 1950s, Maslow introduced one of the most influential ideas in psychology: humans don't just want to survive — we want to 'become'.

Maslow called this drive **self-actualization**: the urge to express your potential, explore your talents, and become the most "you" version of yourself.

Maslow was 46 years old in 1954 when he described self-actualization as:

> *"What a man can be, he must be.*
> *This need we may call self-actualization."*

Abraham Maslow, Motivation and Personality (1954)

Of course, today it would be what a 'person' can be, they must be.... But the message is the same. It's not about fixing something broken — it's about unlocking what already exists inside you.

Maslow defined self-actualization as the fulfillment of one's unique potential — becoming everything you're capable of becoming. It's the process of realizing and expressing your full self, in your own way, on your own terms.

Self-actualization isn't about fixing something broken.
It's about unlocking what already exists inside you.

Maslow said self-actualization looks like:

- Creativity
- Pursuing meaningful goals
- Living authentically
- Feeling moments of joy or insight
- Growing because it feels right
- Exercising autonomy — choosing your own path

Maslow's original five-tier hierarchy included:

1. Physiological needs (food, water, sleep)
2. Safety (housing, health, stability)

3. Love and belonging (connection, family, friendship)

4. Esteem (achievement, confidence, self-respect)

5. Self-actualization (fulfilling your potential)

Later in life, in the late 1960s, he added a sixth and final tier:

Self-transcendence

The desire to go beyond personal growth and contribute to something greater than yourself.

This is where the 10% Project really shines.

It starts with your personal curiosity, courage, and creativity... and it almost always grows outward — into community, impact, and service.

You grow → and then you give. One small step at a time.

Where Your 10% Project Lives in Maslow's Pyramid

Your 10% Project naturally lives in the self-actualization layer:

- Personal growth
- Creativity
- Exploration
- Passion pursuit
- Developing your voice
- Becoming fully yourself

But it also strengthens the layers beneath it:

- Boosting esteem by building confidence, competence, and mastery

- Creating belonging through mentorship, community, or teamwork

- Even improving safety by opening new opportunities, skills, or career paths which can increase financial security

And beautifully, it often becomes self-transcendence:

- Projects that lift others

- Creativity that inspires

- Courage that becomes contagious

- Growth that becomes generosity

Your spark becomes the lantern.

Maslow's Hierarchy of Needs & The 10% Project

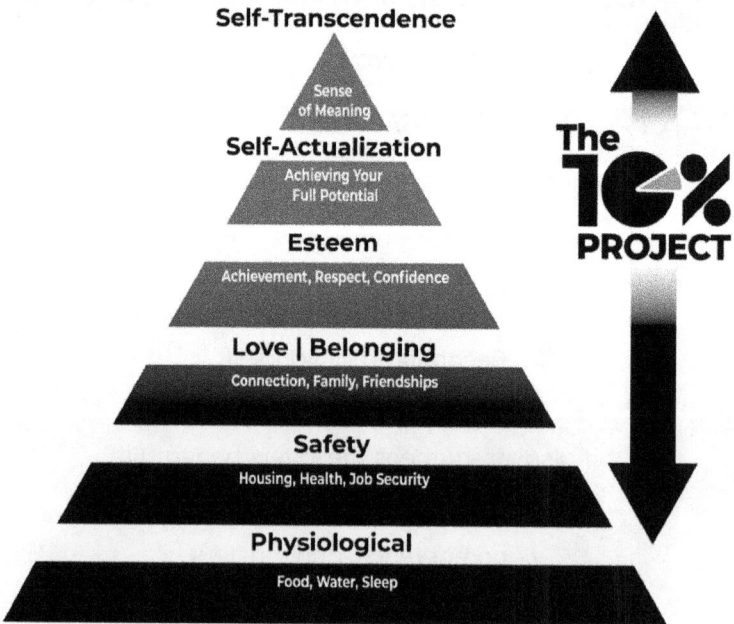

Self-Transcendence

Sense of Meaning

Self-Actualization

Achieving Your Full Potential

Esteem

Achievement, Respect, Confidence

Love | Belonging

Connection, Family, Friendships

Safety

Housing, Health, Job Security

Physiological

Food, Water, Sleep

The **10%** PROJECT

Then in the 1970's Motivational Psychology evolved....

Self-Determination Theory (SDT)

Maslow mapped the big picture. But decades later, psychologists wanted to understand the *daily* psychological forces that actually fuel human motivation.

In the late 1970s through the 1990s, psychologists **Edward Deci and Richard Ryan** developed **Self-Determination Theory (SDT)** — now one of the most widely researched motivation theories in the world.

If Maslow's Hierarchy of Needs explains **what humans long for**, Self-Determination Theory explains **what keeps us moving.**

Self-Determination Theory says **humans thrive** when **three basic psychological needs** are met:

1. **Autonomy**
   Feeling you're making choices that reflect who you are.

2. **Competence**
   Feeling capable, growing, and making progress.

3. **Relatedness**
   Feeling connected to others, supported, and part of something.

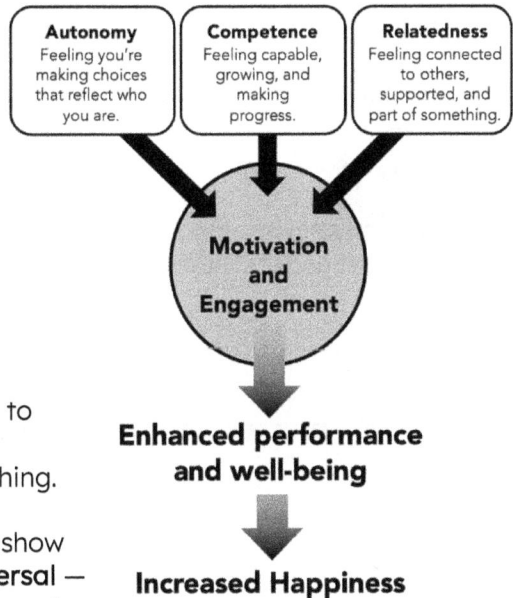

Decades of research show these needs are **universal** — across ages, cultures, and socioeconomic backgrounds.

Autonomy
Feeling you're making choices that reflect who you are.

Competence
Feeling capable, growing, and making progress.

Relatedness
Feeling connected to others, supported, and part of something.

Motivation and Engagement

Enhanced performance and well-being

Increased Happiness

Here's the cool thing:
A 10% Project naturally supports all three.

Autonomy

- You choose your spark and the 10% Project you want to pursue
- You choose your steps – one small step at a time
- It's your direction, not someone else's agenda

Competence

- Tiny actions build skill, momentum, and confidence
- You feel yourself getting stronger, more skilled, and more competent

Relatedness

- Projects pull in mentors, collaborators, supporters, and cheerleaders.
- Growth creates connection.

This is why tiny actions (Hops), structured guidance (The 10% Project 7 Steps), and real movement (Jumping into action) feel so energizing:

They directly satisfy the three psychological needs Self-Determination Theory identifies.

This is why 10% Projects don't feel like "extra work."

They feel like **psychological nourishment**.

How the 10% Project taps into Self-Determination Theory (SDT)

Here are some examples showing how the 10% Project's seven step framework maps to the Self-Determination Theory. As a framework, every step supports Autonomy, Competency and Relatedness in unique ways.

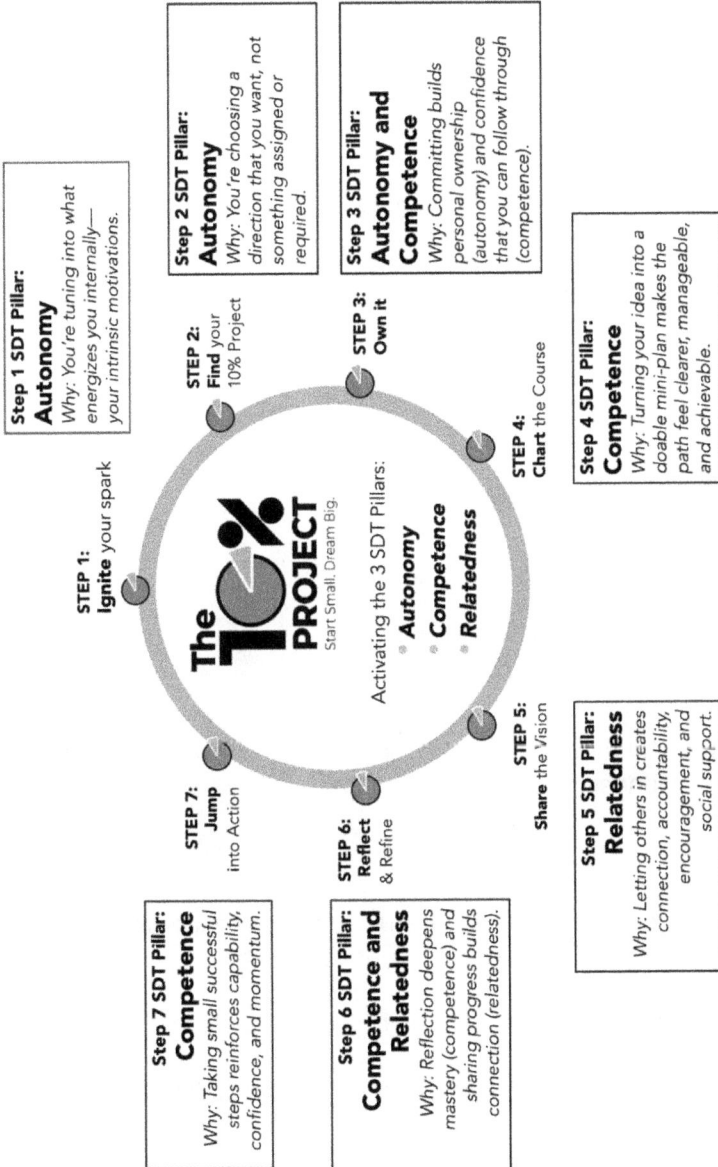

STEP 1: Ignite your spark

Step 1 SDT Pillar: **Autonomy**
Why: You're tuning into what energizes you internally— your intrinsic motivations.

STEP 2: Find your 10% Project

Step 2 SDT Pillar: **Autonomy**
Why: You're choosing a direction that you want, not something assigned or required.

STEP 3: Own it

Step 3 SDT Pillar: **Autonomy and Competence**
Why: Committing builds personal ownership (autonomy) and confidence that you can follow through (competence).

STEP 4: Chart the Course

Step 4 SDT Pillar: **Competence**
Why: Turning your idea into a doable mini-plan makes the path feel clearer, manageable, and achievable.

STEP 5: Share the Vision

Step 5 SDT Pillar: **Relatedness**
Why: Letting others in creates connection, accountability, encouragement, and social support.

STEP 6: Reflect & Refine

Step 6 SDT Pillar: **Competence and Relatedness**
Why: Reflection deepens mastery (competence) and sharing progress builds connection (relatedness).

STEP 7: Jump into Action

Step 7 SDT Pillar: **Competence**
Why: Taking small successful steps reinforces capability, confidence, and momentum.

The **10% PROJECT**
Start Small. Dream Big.

Activating the 3 SDT Pillars:
- Autonomy
- Competence
- Relatedness

Accessible for Everyone

This is also why the 10% Project is accessible
(...and not just for people with privilege).

Because autonomy, competence, and connection are
not luxuries — they're human needs.

A 10% Project doesn't require:

- money
- loads of free time
- a perfect schedule
- fancy tools
- a certain job
- a certain background

It only requires:

- a spark
- curiosity
- the courage to begin
- small, doable actions
- and **YOU**

This is why the 10% Project works across all socioeconomic
backgrounds.

It grows from psychological needs that every human shares.

Maslow explains the need for realizing and expressing your
full self, in your own way, on your own terms.

Self-Determination Theory tells us what fuels the journey.

The 10% Project gives you a practical way to live both —
every day.

With each small step, you build:

- Autonomy
- Competence
- Connection
- Esteem
- Belonging
- Creativity
- Meaning
- Contribution

This is how **self-actualization becomes self-transcendence.**
How personal growth becomes community growth.
How lighting your spark creates light for others too.

A Lived Example: Why I Believe This Works

I want to pause here and say something important.

I didn't set out to write a psychology-backed framework.
I didn't sit down and say, *"Let me design something that perfectly aligns with Maslow and Self-Determination Theory."*

I just started and I learned more with every small step.

For decades, I've taken small steps toward things that mattered to me—often without a plan, without certainty, and definitely without calling it "theory." I followed curiosity. I experimented. I learned as I went.

Only as I got to the point of looking back over my career, I realized something surprising: I've been running 10% Projects my whole life.

And once I understood the psychology behind motivation, something clicked. I could finally see *why* this approach works so well—not just for me, but for so many people I'd watched do the same thing.

So let me make this real...

A Real 10% Project in Action: This Book

I didn't set out to write a book.
I hadn't written one before.
I didn't have a plan to publish.
I wasn't sure where to start.
I certainly didn't feel "ready."

"The 10% Project" started as a tiny spark—a single slide in a presentation. Just one idea I couldn't stop thinking about.

But instead of waiting until I felt qualified, confident, or certain, I took one small step... And then another.

That's how this book happened—not through a grand plan, but through small 10% steps, repeated again, and again.

Now, looking back, I can see how this 10% Project – my first book titled "The 10% Project" - quietly activated everything Maslow and Self-Determination Theory describe:

- Autonomy
- Competence
- Connection
- Esteem
- Belonging
- Creativity
- Meaning
- Contribution

Certainly not because I engineered it that way—but because that's how human growth actually works.

Autonomy: *I Chose the Spark*

No one assigned me this project. No one told me I had to do it. I just followed a question that wouldn't leave me alone:

Why do projects with small, brave steps create opportunity and change people?

I chose the direction.
I chose the pace.
I chose to begin... before I felt confident.

That's autonomy—not freedom from responsibility,
but ownership of direction.

Competence: *Tiny Steps Built Real Confidence*

I didn't wake up knowing how to write, and then publish, a book. I learnt as I went.

I learned by writing.
I learned by sharing drafts and asking questions.
Lots and lot of questions.
I learned by teaching before I felt "qualified."

Each small step made the next one easier.
Each iteration built real skill—not imagined confidence.
Competence didn't come first. *Action did.*

Connection (Relatedness): *The Project Pulled People In*

As the idea for this book grew, so did the relationships around it.

- Mentors.
- Students.
- Colleagues.
- Friends who said, *"This helped me."*

The "Project" created connection—not the other way around.

I didn't set out to build a community.
I shared something I cared about, and connection followed.

Belonging: *Finding Your Place by Showing Up*

Belonging wasn't something I chased.
It emerged as I showed up consistently.

By sharing unfinished ideas.
By teaching while learning.
By letting the work be seen before it was perfect.

I didn't try to *fit in*—I let myself contribute.
And through contribution, 'belonging' naturally formed.

Esteem: *Confidence Came from Doing, Not Proving*

This wasn't about external validation or credentials.
It was about quiet self-trust.

Each step reinforced a simple belief:

> *"I can figure things out as I go."*

That kind of esteem doesn't come from titles.
It comes from keeping promises to yourself.

Creativity: *Letting the Work Evolve*

Creativity didn't arrive as a lightning bolt—it was permission
I gave myself to just start and learn as I went.

- Permission to experiment.
- Permission to revise.
- Permission to let the idea change shape over time.

This book became real because it wasn't locked into a perfect first version. Creativity flourishes when the stakes stay small.

The structure of small steps created room to explore, test, revise, and play. Creativity thrives when the pressure to be perfect is removed.

10% Projects don't demand brilliance.
They invite curiosity.

Even as I add these new pages (I think it is about the 6th update to this book) I keep learning and the book keeps evolving.

Meaning: *When the Work Starts to Matter*

At some point, this book stopped being "something I was trying" and started being something that mattered.

Not because it was big.
But because it was aligned.

- Aligned with my values.
- Aligned with what energized me.
- Aligned with what helped others.

Meaning didn't arrive all at once.
It accumulated—one small step at a time.

Contribution: *When Growth Turns Outward*

It all started with a single slide titled "The 10% Project"
a personal career insight shared with students in an
executive MBA program...
Which led to deeper conversations...
Leading to a framework – a guide others could follow...
Evolving into presentations,
Becoming a book...
and now...

... The 10% Project is an official program I am teaching at **Stanford University.**

An outcome that, when I started this crazy journey 12 months ago, I could never have imagined in my wildest dreams.

None of this evolved because I had a master plan.
It happened because I kept taking the next 10% step.
Personal growth quietly became contribution.

This is how self-actualization becomes self-transcendence.

We start by exploring what lights us up, and almost without trying, it begins to create light for others too.

Has writing this book, The 10% Project, made me happier and more fulfilled.... Yes!

Why This Works for Everyone

Decades of research behind Self-Determination Theory show that autonomy, competence, and relatedness are **universal human needs**.

They apply:

- across ages
- across cultures
- across socioeconomic backgrounds

These are not luxuries reserved for people with time, money, or access. The principles are fundamental human psychological drivers. Anyone, absolutely anyone, can use 10% Projects to create opportunity for themselves.

This has honestly been one of the most exciting insights for me. The concept of a 10% Project is available for anyone, at any stage of life and, by activating the three pillars of the Self Determination Theory, has the potential to make anyone's life better, happier, more fulfilled.

That's why a 10% Project doesn't require:

- money
- perfect conditions
- a certain job
- a certain background

10% Project are motivating because the psychology is human – and common across all people, cultures, societies and socioeconomic groups.

A Lived Experience - Not Theory on a Page.

The 10% Project works because it aligns with how humans, you and I, actually grow.

We don't need a breakthrough.
We don't need permission.
We don't need to reinvent our lives.

We just need:

- A spark
- Curiosity
- A first small step, and
- The courage to begin before we're ready

A 10% Project isn't self-help.

It's a tool for self-activation.

And the psychology simply explains what many of us already know deep down:

When we take one small, brave step toward something that matters to us, everything else starts to move with us.

CHAPTER 4:

Why 10% Projects Always Work

10% Projects always work—Always... not because they guarantee success, but because they always guarantee growth. Whether they soar or stall, they generate energy and value that moves you forward towards your personal goals.

Even if a project takes an unexpected turn or doesn't unfold the way you planned, the process itself becomes the payoff. You build momentum, clarity, and confidence—all essential for personal and professional growth

Yep—even if your project falls flat, fizzles out, or never sees the light of day!

Why? Because the true value of a 10% Project lives in the *doing*—the learning 'hops' you make along the way, not the final result alone. You flex new muscles, push your thinking, and shift how others perceive you, simply by taking initiative.

The reality is that great ideas stall for all sorts of reasons.

- Maybe the brilliance isn't recognized right away.
- Maybe the timing is off.
- Maybe your idea hits the wall of office politics.
- Budgets are cut.
- Your current leadership changes.
- Or you didn't have all the data you needed.

Even the best ideas can flop. But 10% Projects aren't about avoiding failure—they're about building the capacity to act, learn, and adapt in real time.

The Power of a 10% Project

The power of a 10% Project is that it shifts your mindset from passive to **proactive**. It tells the world—*and yourself*—that you're someone who doesn't wait for change, you create it.

And here's the magic: even if your idea doesn't land, the fact that you tried sets you apart. People notice. They remember. That shift in perception can unlock new and exciting doors for you.

The Process Matters More Than the Result

When you start intentionally scanning your environment for ways to make it better—especially if you've felt stuck or resigned to "how things are"—you activate a new lens. Suddenly, problems become puzzles. Frustrations turn into fuel. You begin to see what *could be* instead of just what *is*.

You shift from observer to driver. Instead of waiting for someone else to fix things, you step up, take the wheel, and steer. That mindset alone changes how you feel about your work—and how others see and experience you.

This shift affects more than your day-to-day tasks. It impacts your energy, your confidence, even your sense of purpose. You feel more engaged, more motivated, and more optimistic—***not because your circumstances changed... because you changed yourself.***

When you choose to drive your growth through a 10% Project, you naturally start gravitating toward work that feels meaningful. You're not just checking boxes anymore—you're designing your path, one small win at a time.

That engagement? It creates a ripple effect. You might gain new skills, deepen relationships, find hidden talents, or even stumble upon a future career pivot. At a minimum, you'll feel more fulfilled—and that alone is worth it.

Taking ownership flips the script. Instead of reacting to change, you become the one initiating it. That proactive mindset compounds over time—and it becomes one of your most valuable career and life assets.

When you're intentional in choosing your 10% Project—picking something that aligns with your values or aspirations—you start to build bridges that lead somewhere meaningful.

And here's the beauty of 10% Projects: *you're in control.* No one assigns them. You get to follow your curiosity and passion in small actional hops—while still building toward something real. That freedom allows you to choose experiences, skills, and relationships that point in the direction you actually want to grow—no detours, no waiting for permission. Just forward movement.

Learning from Setbacks

Sometimes, even with your best intentions, effort, and energy, a 10% Project might veer off course. It's tempting to label that a failure—but don't. These moments are often the richest learning opportunities in disguise.

Even when things don't work out, the value doesn't vanish. You'll have stretched new muscles, gained experience, expanded your network, and met people who now associate you with action, initiative, and positive momentum. You become known—not just as someone with ideas, but someone who *does things.* And that reputation sticks.

Take a beat and ask yourself: What worked? What didn't? What would I do differently next time? This kind of honest reflection is what turns a misstep into a masterclass.

The truth is that the skill of extracting wisdom from setbacks might be the most underrated superpower in your professional toolkit. It builds resilience, humility, and insight—and those qualities compound over every future project you take on.

The Real Opportunity: Changing Perceptions.

Frustrated with archaic reporting systems at work, a colleague launched a 10% Project to streamline the existing clunky monthly reporting process. They researched solutions, mapped out a better flow, even tested it with a few colleagues. In the end, the new system didn't catch on—maybe it wasn't the right fit, or the team wasn't ready to adopt it. But here's the thing: their initiative didn't go unnoticed. Colleagues saw their problem-solving mindset. Leaders saw their drive. And when the next high-visibility opportunity came around, guess who was top of mind? It wasn't the quiet bystander—it was the person who raised their hand and tried something bold.

Whether your 10% Project succeeds, stalls, or lands somewhere in between, one thing is certain: you'll be better off than if you hadn't tried. You'll have sharpened your instincts, deepened relationships, reshaped how others see you—and perhaps most importantly, proven to yourself that you're the kind of person who *takes initiative.* That confidence carries over to every challenge you take on moving forward.

The process of doing a 10% Project will drive change, in the way you think, the skills you have, the people you know... perhaps it will even help bring clarity to your current role and your ambition to achieve more, inside or outside your current position.

Moving Forword

Once your 10% Project wraps, don't just move on—*mine the gold.* Reflect on what you learned. What surprised you? What energized you? Where did you stretch the most? Thank the people who helped you along the way. Document those lessons and the ripple effects they created.

Each project adds another piece to your bigger puzzle. These small wins build up, and over time, they shape the trajectory of your personal and professional life. You're not just taking action—you're building momentum.

Remember: the real win isn't just finishing a project. It's cultivating a mindset—one that welcomes challenge, chases growth, and learns through doing.

In that mindset, you're no longer just doing the day-to-day work—you're *architecting your future.* One project at a time, you're designing a life that reflects your values, your creativity, and your drive.

This proactive energy is magnetic. It positions you as someone who not only dreams up good ideas—you actually make them happen. And that kind of energy? It spreads. People want to work with it, support it, and be around it.

The best part? Once this mindset clicks, it becomes second nature. And like any good habit, it continues to move you forward—project by project, breakthrough by breakthrough.

CHAPTER 5

But I Don't Have Time!

Let's be real—almost no one feels like they have extra time lying around. Life is already busy: work, family, errands, obligations. So how on earth are you supposed to *add* a 10% Project to your already overflowing plate? If you're thinking, "Sounds great, but I'm just too busy," you're not alone. That's the most common pushback I hear—and I've said it myself more than once.

But here's the truth: if you want change, you have to create space for it. Opportunity doesn't fall into your lap while you're scrolling though social media or rewatching old movies—it shows up when you *make space* for it. And while finding time isn't always easy, it's far more possible than most people realize. Once you shift from "I don't have time" to "How can I make time?", you'll start seeing hidden pockets of opportunity all over the place.

The Real Challenge: Prioritizing Time

As a VP in a fast-paced Silicon Valley startup, with an active daughter, Gabby—a busy teenager in middle school—I totally get the "no time" challenge on a deeply personal level. Even with an incredibly supportive husband, there are many days I feel like I'm sprinting just to stay upright. Time is always tight. Downtime feels mythical.

In fact, this book—my very own 10% Project—was mostly written in the margins of my life. I typed chapters while sitting on the floor outside Gabby's ballet classes, during long-haul flights for work, and in the passenger seat on family road trips.

I used to laugh at my own dream of writing a book. "Who has time for that?!" For years, I convinced myself I might do it someday—after retirement, when things quieted down.

It was the challenge from Liz, that ambitious MBA student, that forced me to rethink. If I wanted to do this—really do this—I couldn't wait for time to magically appear. I had to prioritize it, protect it, and claim it as mine.

Writing a book had always been one of those quiet dreams— the kind you carry in the back of your mind but never give yourself permission to pursue. Sure, I hoped people would read it. Maybe I'd land a speaking gig or two. But more than that, I wanted to prove to myself that I could turn a long-held dream into reality.

The real motivator? Proving to myself that I had something to say—and the grit to say it. So I did the scariest and most powerful thing you can do when time feels scarce: I made the project matter enough to rearrange things around it. I reprioritized my most limited resource: time. And that choice changed everything.

Life can be exhausting. With everything going on in the world today and the constant bombardment of news and opinions 24 hours a day, where do you find time to step off life's metaphorical treadmill and take a breath.

The answer will be different for everyone. Let me tell you how I started down my 10% Project path for this book.

Weekend Retreat: My Saturday Ritual

Every Saturday, my daughter Gabby, immerses herself in four to five hours of ballet—her passion, her happy place.

I could have easily dropped her off, run errands, or headed home for a breather. But instead, I stayed at the studio. I found a quiet little spot to sit and work. A spot, over time, that staff there began affectionately calling "my office."

That space became sacred to me. A place I focused on what was important to me. While other parents chatted, or scrolled through their phones, I would crack open my laptop. I wasn't trying to write a best-seller—I was just carving out something of my own. Those chunks of focused time, paired with the occasional midday snack break with my daughter, became gold.

And honestly? It wasn't just about the book. It was about choosing to be fully present—for my daughter and for myself. I could have been endlessly scrolling, numbing out, passing the time. Instead, I turned those Saturdays into a quiet ritual of creation. Six months later, I had a full draft in hand. That wasn't luck—it was small, steady intention stacked up over time.

Finding Your Own "Time Pockets"

No ballet class? No problem. Everyone has their own version of "hidden time." Maybe it's your train commute. Maybe it's that hour while your child is at soccer practice. Maybe it's the lull before dinner or those few minutes in the school pickup line. Those little windows might not seem like much —but together, they can become the runway for your 10% Project.

A great place to start? Take a look at your daily habits— especially the sneaky ones that consume time without giving much back. That's where you'll often find your biggest wins.

Social Media

This one was a big wake-up call for me. I could lose entire chunks of my day to the social media vortex—swiping through political debates, cat videos, celebrity gossip I wasn't really even interested in. The hours slipped by quietly, disguised as relaxation.

My personal weakness? Taylor Swift videos. So many. So sparkly. So... endless. And let's be honest—she *is* amazing. But eventually, I had to stop and ask, "Is this moving the needle on anything I care about?" The answer was no. So I made the switch—I started trading scroll time for project time. Not every minute, but enough to feel the shift.

Television and Videos

We're living in the golden age of streaming—so much content, so little time. From YouTube rabbit holes to Netflix sagas, there's *always* something new to watch. And I'm not saying it's bad—great stories can inspire and entertain.

I love a juicy series as much as anyone. But now, I give myself boundaries. Cutting down on Netflix isn't about sacrifice—it's about choice. And let's face it, maybe you don't need to watch every season of that dating show where no one ends up together anyway. You can still enjoy your favorite escapes *and* make room for something that's yours—your project, your growth—it's your turn.

Online Gaming

Gaming isn't my personal vice, but I know for many people it's a full-on lifestyle. And hey, if it brings you joy, go for it! But ask yourself—could you carve out 30 minutes here or there for something else you care about? It's not about giving up what you love. It's about choosing to diversify how you invest your energy.

Watching Sports

And to all the sports fans—you're safe here. No one's asking you to skip the playoffs. But maybe in the off-season, or during halftime, you could chip away at your 10% Project. It's about shifting just a little attention toward what *you* want to build.

Airplane Productivity

Let's talk travel. As someone who flies often—sometimes halfway around the world—I've learned that airplane time is secret gold. While others queue up back-to-back movies or double down on free wine, I open my laptop.

No judgment—movies and naps have their place. But I choose to invest that quiet, uninterrupted time into something that fills *me* up. And you know what? I land feeling clearer, sharper, and one step further ahead than when I boarded.

It's About Balance

This isn't about living on a mountain with no Wi-Fi or cutting out everything you enjoy. It's about awareness.

When you know where your time really goes, you can make smarter, more empowering choices — *without giving up the things that bring you joy.*

Love your shows? Can't miss a game? Obsessed with your favorite feed? Great—keep those! But maybe... just maybe... carve out a sliver of time from each and give it to something that fuels your growth. That small shift can drive big momentum.

Even if it doesn't feel like it, most of us have way more flexible time than we think—we've just programmed it into default habits. A 10% Project challenges you to reclaim those moments and redirect them toward something that really matters to *you.*

Do a quick mental audit: how much time are you giving away without realizing it? Scrolling. Streaming. Swiping. Gaming. It adds up. You don't have to ditch all your leisure—but being honest about how much time it eats is the first step to getting some of it back.

When your phone tells you how much screen time you've had and you squirm a little and look away, make a choice if that is really the best way to use your time.

Try swapping just *one* hour of screen time this week for your 10% Project. That's it. One hour. Perhaps 20 minutes a day works better for you. Do that for a month, and you'll be amazed at what you've built. The compound effect is real— you'll be amazed at what you can do in that focused 10 hours a month dedicated towards an idea that is meaningful to you, and it starts with one small trade.

Making Time Work for You

We all need downtime. We all recharge in different ways. But you can unwind *and* still make space to grow—if you're intentional. That's the difference.

Whether it's on a commute, in a waiting room, during your lunch break, or right before bed—use those little pockets of time. Micro-moments and every little hop forward matters.

The Daily Commute: Turning Dead Time into Dream Time

For years, my 35-minute commute each way to and from work was just... dead time. I'd sing along to the radio, memorize all the words to my favorite songs, and sure — it passed the time. But it didn't energize me. It didn't build anything new.

So, I made one small shift: I started calling friends.

One friend in particular, Michael (you'll meet him in this book!), became my unofficial morning co-pilot. Almost every other day, we'd dive into conversations about new ideas, 10% Projects, and ways we could shake things up. Those calls didn't just fill the time — they sparked real energy and new opportunities. Some of his projects even grew into full-blown launches.

And when I'm not talking to Michael, I call someone else in my network — just to say hello, to check in, to catch up. The best time to build your network is before you need anything. A simple, genuine check-in can turn even a ten-minute window into a chance to see if a friend needs help, inspiration, or might just be an opportunity to strengthen a foundation for future connection.

Small shifts in how you use your time can change everything.

It's All About Intentionality

Time won't politely knock and say, "Hey, here's a free hour!" It doesn't just appear—you *claim* it. That means taking a real look at where your time is leaking and asking, "What can I swap, shift, or pause?" Every intentional choice adds fuel to the future you want.

At the end of the day, this isn't about waiting for the mythical "perfect time" to begin. It's about being intentional, creative, and just a little stubborn with the time you *do* have. Time isn't fixed—it's flexible. Once you realize you can bend it toward your goals, everything changes.

"Good fortune is what happens
when opportunity
meets with planning."

Thomas Edison

SECTION 3
7 Simple Steps for Implementation

CHAPTER 6

Welcome to the Framework

Seven Simple Steps

It's time to get your hands dirty—in the best way possible. This section is your toolkit. We're breaking down the full 10% Project process into seven simple, clear, doable steps so you can go from *idea* to *impact* with confidence.

STEP 1: Ignite Your Spark

STEP 2: Find Your 10% Project

STEP 3: Own it

STEP 4: Chart the Course

STEP 5: Share the Vision

STEP 6: Reflect and Refine

STEP 7: Jump Into Action

The 10% PROJECT
Start Small. Dream Big.

Seven Simple Steps

Let's get one thing clear up front: this is not a theory book. It's a *do something with it* book.

The 10% Project isn't about overhauling your life or waiting for the "right time" (*spoiler alert: that time never comes*).

It's about taking a small slice of your time and using it with bold, intentional energy. This framework — these seven steps — are not rules. They're scaffolding. A structure you can lean on while you build something that matters.

And here's the best part: everything you need is already inside you.

This framework won't give you purpose — **you bring the purpose.**

What the framework gives you is:

- Traction.
- Focus.
- Movement.

Each step is designed to meet you where you are — busy, skeptical, hopeful, overwhelmed, inspired, all of it. This is life-friendly. Whether you're feeling on fire or barely lit, there's a place to begin.

And that place is a 'Hop'.

A tiny, doable action — five minutes, ten minutes, fifteen at most — that gets you moving without pressure or perfection. Hops are how small ideas, become bigger plans, and then big ideas, becoming real momentum.

Do what you can.

Start small.
Take one Hop.
And then another.

SEVEN SIMPLE STEPS | 75

Let these next chapters be your guide, your nudge, your mirror.

One spark at a time, one hop at a time, one step at a time — this is how we begin.

Welcome to the 10% Project.
Let's get moving.

CHAPTER 7

STEP 1: Ignite Your Spark

The first step? Zoom in on what *really* matters to you. What fires you up? What grinds your gears so much you wish you could fix it today? Where do you feel stuck, or secretly curious? Maybe it's your job, your community, your routine, or your lack of creative outlet. Whatever it is—name it. This is the fuel for your 10% Project.

THINK ABOUT YOUR PERSONAL GOALS

One of my favorite quotes comes from *Alice in Wonderland*, when Alice asks the Cheshire Cat, *"Which road should I take?"* and he replies, *"Well, where are you going?"* When she says, *"I don't know,"* he simply says, *"Then it doesn't matter. If you don't know where you're going, any road will take you there."* That's the trap we fall into when we don't define our direction. Without clarity, any path *feels* valid—but most likely none of them lead us to the outcomes we really want. That's why this step matters. Defining your goals upfront helps you filter, focus, and make every move count.

Where are you going?

Now, take a beat and reflect: What excites you? What's missing in your current life or career? Maybe you've got the skills but no hands-on experience. Maybe you've got passion but no network. A 10% Project is your bridge—the thing that closes the gap between where you are and where you want to go.

There's no "one right goal." The beauty of a 10% Project is that it can flex to support *your* ambitions—whatever they are.

But the clearer you are about what you want, the more powerful your 10% Project will be. Don't rush this step. Give your dream some space to breathe.

Defining your destination gives your 10% Project direction. Without it, you risk working hard but getting nowhere meaningful. With it, you build momentum that actually takes you somewhere that *matters.*

There are whole books written about finding your passion. This isn't one of them.

I'm not going to ask you to take a two-week silent retreat or draft a 50-page life manifesto (unless you want to!).

Instead, this is a fast-track — a quick, practical way to spot your sparks, connect the dots, and start building a 10% Project (or even a full career) around them.

Finding Your Spark

Before you can build a 10% Project — or create the kind of momentum that shifts your life — you need a spark.

- Not a fully formed plan.
- Not a grand vision.
- Just a flicker of energy.

What is a Spark?

A spark is that small but unmistakable pull — a feeling of excitement, curiosity, or even a little frustration — that creates energy. It's that moment when you find yourself leaning forward, your brain clicking faster, or your heart beating just a little harder.

- It doesn't have to be big.
- It doesn't have to be polished.
- It just has to light you up, even for a moment.

Where to Find It:

You don't have to invent your spark from scratch. It's already hiding in plain sight:

- Hobbies or interests you lose yourself in.
- Problems you wish someone would solve.
- Compliments you keep getting but maybe haven't taken seriously.
- Conversations where you feel more alive than usual.

Your spark might come from something you already love — or something that quietly annoys you so much that you feel pulled to fix it. Either way, it's a clue.

Often things that seem so easy to you, are easy because you have a unique passion for them. Often we overlook these sparks or ideas as something we believe anyone can do simply because they are so natural to us. We forget that everyone has different innate skills, something simple for you might be exactly what someone else desperately needs help with or are intimidated to tackle themselves.

If you need some inspiration, the Spark Deck™ is a tool that can help you discover what energizes you and helps you to identify your Spark Zone— ready to turn it into aligned action. The Spark Deck, contains over 70 Spark Cards that are used throughout The 10% Project framework to help you clarify what lights you up and where to begin. Sort, reflect, and unlock patterns that lead to projects with purpose. Find them on The 10% Project website.

The Goal:

This isn't about finding your "one true calling" (no pressure!). It's about gathering clues — enough to take a step forward. Enough to try, explore, and build. Because clarity comes from action, not from sitting around waiting for a lightning bolt.

The magic of a 10% Project isn't about having everything figured out. It's about trusting that small sparks, when nurtured, can ignite something bigger than you ever imagined.

Once you've found a few sparks...
You can start connecting the dots.

1: List Your Energy Sources

Think about when you've felt most energized — excited, curious, passionate, or even just deeply focused.

Where does your mind naturally wander when you aren't being told what to do?

Write down anything that feels real:

- Helping others
- Designing things
- Solving puzzles
- Building communities
- Organizing chaos
- Learning new ideas
- Fixing broken systems

And yes — even the things that annoy you can be energy sources! If it fires you up, it's worth noting.

2: Identify Core Themes

Now step back. Look for patterns. Do your sparks cluster around certain types of action or impact?

Common spark themes often include:

- Creating
- Leading
- Connecting
- Building
- Solving
- Helping
- Expressing

You might find two or three major threads that keep showing up. That's a good sign — you're getting warmer.

3: Connect Passion to Possibility

Now start imagining:

- How could these themes show up in a 10% Project?
- Could they hint at career pivots, side businesses, or personal growth areas?

You're not locking yourself into a forever-plan.
You're just opening doors.

- Maybe your love of helping people could turn into mentoring others.
- Maybe your obsession with systems could spark a project improving team workflows.
- Maybe your creative energy could fuel a branding refresh that gets you noticed.
- Small steps. Big shifts. That's the goal.

Aligning Your Spark with Action

Finding your spark is only the beginning. The real magic happens when you act on it.

Small Moves, Big Momentum

You don't have to quit your job or overhaul your whole life tomorrow. Just take that first small step.

A 10% Project lets you explore your sparks safely — testing ideas in a low-risk, high-growth way. You get to experiment, learn, adjust, and grow — without blowing everything up.

Example Paths: Here are a few ways sparks can show up through small 10% Projects:

- Love helping people? Mentor junior team members or new hires.
- Obsess over design? Volunteer to refresh your company's lunch area decorations or event materials.
- Hate inefficient systems? Propose a small pilot project to streamline a workflow or process.

Each move is a steppingstone. Not just toward what you want — but toward discovering what lights you up even more. Reminder: Finding your spark isn't always a loud "aha!" moment.

It's often a quiet curiosity — a gentle pull you notice when you start paying attention.

- Nurture it.
- Trust it.
- Follow it.

Because small steps, fueled by sparks, can lead to new opportunities that align with your passion and create more joy in your life.

CHAPTER 8

STEP 2: Find Your 10% Project

It's time to turn on your "10% radar." You've identified your spark, now you need to find a 10% Project that aligns. A 10% Project that will move you in the direction you want to go. There are opportunities all around you—but most people are too distracted or discouraged to see them. The good news? Once you start looking intentionally, they'll start popping out like neon signs.

LOOK AROUND YOU FOR IDEAS

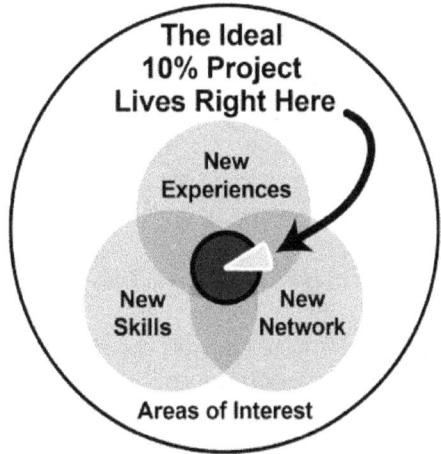

The Ideal
10% Project
Lives Right Here

New
Experiences

New
Skills

New
Network

Areas of Interest

The best 10% Projects create a double benefit: they align with your personal goals *and* help you grow—through new experiences, stronger skills, and expanded connections. If your project does that, you're golden. The most powerful 10% Projects live at the intersection of what *you* care about and what *creates value*—for others, your team, your community, and your future self. **A 10% Project is about you. About your goals and your dreams.**

Choose something that excites you—seriously. If your 10% Project feels like a chore, it'll lose steam fast. You want a project that pulls you in, sparks curiosity, or makes you feel like, "I *have* to try this." **Sparks ignite fires!**

Scan your environment for ideas that hit at least two out of three checkboxes:

- ⬤ Provides the opportunity to learn new skills.
- ⬤ Offers new experiences, and
- ⬤ Connects you to new people or networks.

Hit all three and create meaningful value...that's a bonafide home run.

Need an Idea? Try These:

At Work

Maybe you want to be seen as project manager material, or you're eyeing an overseas assignment. A 10% Project could help you prove your leadership skills or expand your visibility across global teams.

Looking for a New Job

Maybe you're craving a career pivot—into tech, sustainability, UX design, you name it. A project in your target field can help you build experience, test your fit, confirm it is an area you'll love, and connect with others in that world before you make the leap.

At Home

Want to be more present with your kids? Teach them something meaningful? A 10% Project could be volunteering together, starting a shared learning goal, or even building a family "kindness mission."

At College

Want to land a dream internship or start your post-grad network early? Try organizing a campus event, writing a blog series in your field, or launch a mini startup that gets you noticed.

At School

Maybe you're craving a stronger social circle or a sense of purpose. Perhaps you're looking for a way to impress the admissions office at your dream college. Try creating a sustainability club, hosting a student-led fundraiser, or launching a peer-to-peer tutoring service.

In Retirement

Maybe you're ready to give back, but on your terms. Start a mentoring group, teach a skill to teens, or finally explore that cause you've never had time for. A 10% Project keeps you connected and fulfilled—without a full-time commitment.

Don't Settle

If something feels *meh*, don't settle. Your time is too valuable. Keep looking until you find a project that feels worth the effort—and ideally, worth bragging about when it's done.

Ideally, your 10% Project doesn't just light *you* up—it also solves a problem others recognize. When a project adds real value for someone else, it becomes contagious. That's when people start noticing and getting excited too.

Think of it this way: what problem could you solve that would let you show off and add to your initiative, skills, experiences and network—all while building something meaningful?

Maybe it stretches you into a new skill set. Maybe it introduces you to collaborators you'd otherwise never meet. Or maybe it simply helps you deepen your existing network through meaningful, visible action. All of that counts.

By now, you've probably got a few ideas bouncing around.
This tool helps you narrow in and find the one that really fits.

Finding Your 10% Project
Where your goals and interests intersect.

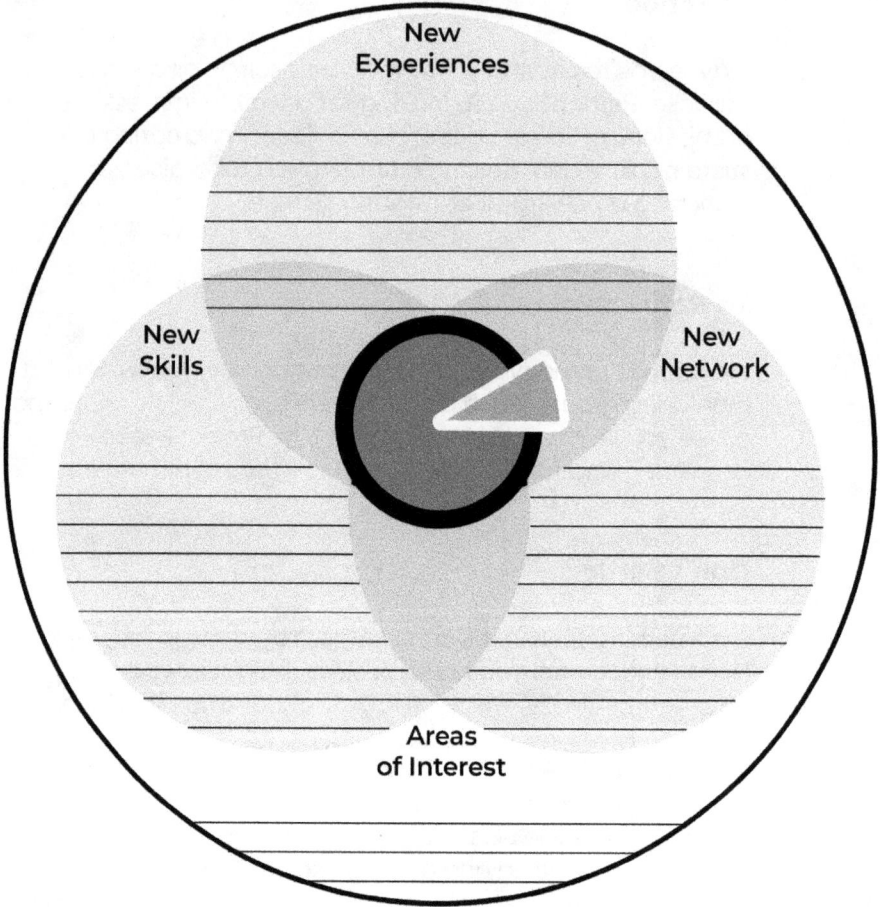

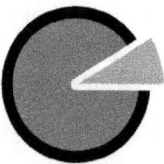

The 10% PROJECT
Start Small. Dream Big.

New
Experiences

New
Skills

New
Network

Areas
of Interest

High level overview of your 10% Project:

Here's the key: a 10% Project isn't about polishing what you're already good at. If you already knock your regular job out of the park, doing it *even better* won't move the needle much. That's maintenance—not momentum.

Real growth and recognition come when you step *outside* the expected—when you surprise people by adding value beyond your job description. That's where the magic (and visibility) happens.

A strong 10% Project reimagines a small part of your world—your life, your work, your community—and brings fresh energy to it. It's not business-as-usual. It's a meaningful *addition* that people notice.

Sometimes that means stepping outside your lane. Stretching. Learning. Feeling a bit uncomfortable. That's where growth and fulfillment live.

A 10% Project is unexpected by design. It's not handed to you—***it's claimed by you***. It lives outside your daily routine. That's what makes it exciting—and impressive.

For example, don't just update that spreadsheet faster—build a new process that eliminates the spreadsheet altogether. That's the kind of initiative that makes people say, "Whoa, that's impressive."

It could be a micro-initiative that solves a recurring pain point, boosts team morale, or builds a resource others didn't even realize they needed—but now can't live without.

Remember—this should be something you *want* to do. Something that energizes you. If your project feels like a burden or a checkbox, it's not the right fit.

Keep going until you find the idea that clicks. It won't feel like an obligation—it'll feel like an *opportunity*. That's your green light.

CHAPTER 9

STEP 3: Own it.

This is where your idea becomes real. Until it's written down, it's just a thought. Documentation makes it tangible, trackable, and impossible to forget. Plus, when your brain is juggling groceries, emails, meetings, and family life, having your 10% Project down in writing is your lifeline.

DOCUMENT, DOCUMENT, DOCUMENT

One thing that may not have occurred to you—writing your ideas down protects your ownership of them. Most of us have had moments where we share a passing thought with a friend or colleague, a process to improve, an idea to increase joy in the workplace, only to find that same idea ends up being implemented by someone else. No more of that. Documentation = proof that you were there first. Document it and then move forward with it to ensure you get the full benefit and value from your great ideas.

Why This Step Matters

Everyone has good ideas. Fewer people write them down. And even fewer take action. Documentation is the gateway to momentum.

Your brain is amazing, but let's be real—it's juggling way too much. Between life admin, chatty coworkers, and surprise calendar invites, your idea deserves a safer home than just your "memory".

Pajamas, Notebooks, and Saving Your Best Ideas (Because "I'll Remember It Later" Never Works)

You know that feeling when you wake up and almost remember a brilliant idea — but it slips away before you can catch it?

Those early-morning, half-awake moments are golden. Your brain is just starting to reengage, that's when some of your most creative, breakthrough thoughts show up.

But seriously — no one's leaping out of bed to fire up a laptop at 5:30 a.m. in their pajamas. (At least, I'm not.)

So here's what I do: I keep a notepad and pen right next to my bed. If something sparks at 3 a.m., I scribble it down without even getting up. It doesn't have to be perfect — it just has to exist outside my half-asleep brain. Because nothing is more frustrating than knowing you had a world-changing idea... and losing it before breakfast.

Writing it down captures the magic before it fades — so when you're fully awake, showered, and ready to take on the day, those brilliant 3 a.m. ideas are still there, waiting for you.

What feels brilliant today might feel blurry tomorrow. Capture that spark before it fades. Write down what you see, feel, and imagine while the fire's still hot.

Documenting your ideas makes them yours

Writing it down sends a clear message: "I'm serious about this." It doesn't matter if it's in a notebook, phone app, or whiteboard photo. The act of documenting gives your idea legitimacy—and *you* authority.

If someone else stumbles across a similar idea later? No problem. You've got your idea captured.

But more than that, documentation helps you explore the idea from multiple angles—and sometimes that's where the *real* gold appears.

You'll almost always see something you hadn't before once you write it out—gaps, patterns, new possibilities. It turns an idea into a blueprint.

Lean into your creativity. Claim your ideas. The process of shaping, scoping, and sharing a 10% Project doesn't just make the project stronger—it changes how people see you. You become "the person who makes things happen."

The world is full of good ideas. What we need more of are people who act. Become that person by moving from concept to commitment. Documentation is the first step.

Documenting your idea kicks off the journey. From here, you'll gain skills, connections, and confidence. You'll learn how to shape vague ideas into clear, compelling action.

People take notice when you treat your ideas seriously. It signals confidence, initiative, and follow-through—the holy trinity of leadership.

When you show you're not just dreaming—you're *doing*—you earn the kind of respect and support that opens doors.

What to Include:

- **Problem or Opportunity:**
  What's the gap you want to close, the problem to fix, or opportunity you're excited about?

- **Challenges:**
  What might get in your way? (list everything—it helps you plan better.)

- **Why it matters:**
  Why is this worth doing? What's at stake if it stays the same?

- **Potential Impact:**
  What could happen if it works? What difference will it make?

- **Approach:**
  What's your plan of attack? Start rough—it doesn't have to be perfect.

The STP (Situation, Target, Proposal) Model

You can use this simple structure to tighten your message:

- **Situation**
  What's the current state?

- **Target**
  What are you aiming to change?

- **Proposal**
  How are you going to do it?

Bottom line? Documenting protects your idea, clarifies your thinking, and gives you the courage to take the next step. Don't skip it. You're building the foundation.

CHAPTER 10

STEP 4: Chart the Course

Lots of people see problems. Fewer suggest solutions. And even fewer *build a plan* to fix them. This is your moment to turn your 10% Project idea into something actionable—something with teeth.

CREATE A STEP-BY-STEP PLAN

It's one thing to toss an idea into a casual conversation. It's another thing to take ownership and say, "I've actually thought this through." A plan turns your good idea into a bold move. It says, *I'm serious.*

You're not just calling out what's broken. You're showing what *better* looks like—and how to get there. That's leadership.

Taking the Lead

This is your moment to show initiative *and* strategic thinking. Spotting a problem is the first step. But building a structured plan to address it? That's next-level. That's what gets you noticed.

Too many great ideas float off into the void—or worse, get scooped up by someone else who gets the spotlight. A plan anchors your idea to *you.*

A thoughtful plan sends a loud message—you're not just full of ideas. You're full of *follow-through.*

Why Planning is Power

A clear plan gives shape to your vision. It breaks the big picture into bite-size pieces. Suddenly, your 10% Project feels less like "someday" and more like "let's go."

It also shows others that you mean business. You're not tossing out half-formed thoughts—you're presenting something structured, credible, and ready to roll.

How to Build Your Plan

Here's a solid starting checklist:

- Break your project into small, doable hops. No overwhelm allowed.
- Identify what you'll need: time, tools, teammates, support.
- Set a few milestone checkpoints to stay on track.
- Draft a timeline—aim for realistic, not perfect.
- Brainstorm roadblocks. How will you navigate around them when they show up?

Plan, but Stay Flexible

Your plan is a map, not a script. Be ready to pivot if you hit roadblocks or discover better options along the way. Flexibility isn't failure—*it's strategy.* Showing that you can adjust course without panicking is a leadership superpower. It earns trust and shows grit.

Example in Action

Say your idea is to streamline a clunky reporting system at work.

Break it down into achievable hops:

- Talk to end users about pain points

- Draft a simple prototype or options list
- Pilot it with a small team
- Collect feedback and refine

Boom—you've got a game plan.

Own the Plan

When you take responsibility for both the idea *and* the execution plan, you step into leadership—even if you're not in charge on paper. Plenty of people have great ideas. Few take that next step. When you do, you stand out—immediately.

Even if your project hits a bump in the road, your willingness to think, plan, and act, puts you in a different category. You become someone who *gets things done*. And people remember that.

The Courage to Commit

The biggest leap is from your *head* to your *hands*. Moving from idea to action takes guts.

World-changers aren't the ones with the most polished ideas. They're the ones who *do something*. Be that person!

Your plan doesn't have to be flawless. It just has to be *real*. It's the difference between dreaming and driving.

Think of your plan like Google Maps: it gives you direction, and adjusts if traffic patterns shift. It doesn't need to be complicated—it just needs to get you moving.

Whether you're reimagining a team process, launching a local event, or testing a startup idea, a solid plan keeps you grounded, confident, and capable. This is how momentum begins. As you grow and evolve... so can your plan

CHAPTER 11

STEP 5: Share the Vision

This is where your idea leaves your notebook and enters the world. But don't blast it out just yet—*timing and delivery* matter more than you think.

SOCIALIZE THE PLAN AND GAIN SUPPORT

Once you've shaped your plan, don't just shout it from the rooftops. Share it *strategically*. Choose your moment—and your people—with care.

Share too soon, and your idea might be misunderstood—or worse, dismissed. Your goal now is gaining traction, not opinions from those who might resent that they weren't the ones who took the initiative.

Start with your trusted circle. The people who'll tell you the truth, ask good questions, and help make your idea stronger—not shoot it down out of fear or ego.

When you're ready and confident, (or can pretend to be), widen your circle to the people who need to know about your 10% Project, *and* the people that you want to know about it.

Pro Tools and Pro Tips

If you're sharing your idea, don't just drop a wall of text. Package it in a way that sparks interest.

Go visual: Use a flowchart, a few PowerPoint slides, or a sketch on a whiteboard. Visuals make your idea feel real and make it easier for others to "get" quickly.

If visuals are your jam, mockup a pitch deck, infographic, or even a simple diagram, give it a name, a logo. It'll help your audience see your vision—and recognize you as someone who has put in serious thought.

A good visual can do in 30 seconds what a paragraph does in 5 minutes. Use that to your advantage.

Clarity = credibility. When people can see it, they can support it. You want them to say, "Wow, this is smart—and doable."

Who Should You Share Your Plan With?

⬤ **Key Decision-Makers**

If your project lives in a work context, loop in your manager or a sponsor early. Getting their buy-in upfront can clear blockers before they appear—and might even earn you visible support.

Engage them early, but only once your concept is solid. Show them it's not just a cool idea—it's a thoughtful solution, with upside for *them* too.

⬤ **Collaborators and Stakeholders**

Think cross-functionally: who else might be impacted, or who could help bring this to life? Invite their ideas and build early ownership.

Getting their input early can foster a sense of ownership and build enthusiasm around the project.

Involving people early makes them feel like co-creators, not just task-doers. That builds momentum—and loyalty.

Plus, they might spot challenges or opportunities you hadn't considered.

And bonus: they'll probably see gaps or shortcuts you didn't. Two brains > one.

People You Want to Impress

Sometimes you want to shine in front of a mentor, executive, or future sponsor. Smart move. Just be sure it's the *right* moment, when the idea is ready for prime time. Sharing your project with the right people can enhance your reputation as a proactive problem-solver.

This is your chance to be seen differently—not just as capable, but as someone who *creates* value. That's a powerful reputation shift.

Subject Matter Experts

Look for people with experience—inside or outside your circle of friends or your company—who've done something similar. Ask questions. Borrow what works.

Their insights could make your idea even better and involving them shows that you value their expertise. Reaching out to experts is a flex—it shows humility, curiosity, and a growth mindset. All big green checks.

This also helps you build a new, more powerful network within the space you're passionate about. You're planting seeds with people who *live everyday* in your area of interest. That network could come in really handy way beyond this one project.

New Voices

Don't be afraid to reach outside your bubble. Use events, or communities to test your idea with new audiences.

Use professional networking tools like LinkedIn to find people with relevant experience or expertise.

A fresh perspective can often cut straight to the insight you didn't know you needed.

You'll be surprised how many people are willing to share their insights and help when you approach them genuinely and without an agenda.

People *love* being asked for their opinion—especially when it feels authentic and not just transactional. You might be surprised how generous people are and how much help they are prepared to give.

Why Sharing is a Smart Strategy

Socializing your project isn't just about getting feedback—it's about creating allies. When people are part of the early process, they're more likely to cheer you on later.

Early buy-in builds traction. Enthusiasm spreads. And when challenges arise, those same people are more likely to help you push through.

Socializing your plan helps to build momentum, and the more invested people are in your success, the easier it becomes to overcome obstacles.

Collaboration > Isolation

Don't try to lone-wolf this – you've already documented your idea, so it is yours. A 10% Project becomes *so much more* when others feel included. You build relationships as you build results.

Inclusion creates champions. People support what they help shape.

And the real win? Collaboration brings ideas you would *never* have thought of alone. That's how good projects become great ones, and great ones become incredible.

Timing is Key

Focus your early conversations on those who have either insight, influence, or impact. Start there—then expand outward. Listen actively. Ask follow-up questions. Show you're coachable and confident at the same time. That combination builds real trust.

CHAPTER 12

STEP 6: Reflect and Refine

Feedback is a gift—use it!

Feedback is your growth accelerator. Treat it like gold—because when you get it, you're one step closer to making your 10% Project bulletproof.

INCORPORATE FEEDBACK AND REFINE

Even the best ideas get sharper when tested with fresh eyes. Stay open. Stay curious. Adjust where it makes sense—and know that refinement isn't weakness. It's leadership.

Bonus: when people see that you *actually use* their input, it builds trust and deepens your relationships. You become known as the person who listens, evolves, and follows through.

Why Feedback Matters

Although we all like hearing it, you really don't need praise—you need perspective. And feedback gives you exactly that. Even a tiny suggestion can reveal a blind spot or unlock a better way forward.

Your idea might be 90% there—but it's that last 10% of clarity, simplicity, or strategy that will make it fly. And you almost never get there without feedback.

Feedback isn't about agreeing with everything. It's about listening deeply, asking questions, and being open to getting even better. That's the mark of someone ready for the next level.

When you seek feedback from experienced voices, you're not just sharpening your project—you're building credibility and expanding your network in the process.

People naturally want to support the person who asks, listens, and grows. You're not just getting advice—you're building allies.

And long-term? You're building a reputation as someone who doesn't just *talk* improvement—you *do* it. That's the kind of person people want to work with and recommend.

People *love* being asked for input—it's a mini compliment. It says: I value your experience. That moment of inclusion builds connection and loyalty.

And when you apply their advice? You've turned a casual contributor into an active supporter. Now they're part of your 10% Project story too.

Be Open to Feedback (Even the Hard Stuff)

Everyone knows feedback can sting. But it's better to hear it early from a supporter than later from a critic.

Even if it catches you off guard, don't dismiss it. Pause. Reflect. There's often a nugget of truth in every comment.

Your new mantra: Curiosity over ego. That's how ideas evolve—and how leaders grow.

Your biggest breakthrough might come from the most unexpected person. That's the magic of staying open.

I Don't Hire Echoes (Why Smart Teams Challenge Each Other)

Whenever someone new joins my team, one of the first things I tell them is simple: "Tell me what you really think."

I don't hire them to nod along. I hire them because they're smart, they see things I might not, and their input could change everything.

My philosophy has always been: If two smart people can't agree on something, there's a reason. Either I know something they don't, or they know something I don't. Either way, we owe it to the project — and to each other — to figure it out.

That only happens when people feel safe enough to speak up. To share different experiences. To offer fresh perspectives. That's where real innovation happens — not in perfect agreement, but in open, honest conversation.

*When someone disagrees with me, I don't take it personally. I lean in. Because whether it helps me catch a blind spot, rethink an idea, or defend my ideas more clearly, either way — **we win.***

Diversity of thought isn't just nice to have. It's the foundation of the best outcomes.

Dealing with Skeptics

Not everyone will get it. That's okay. Some people resist new ideas out of habit, not malice. Be prepared—and stay grounded.

Ask yourself: are they poking holes, or highlighting something you genuinely overlooked? Sometimes pushback makes your idea stronger.

If they raise a real risk—address it. Proactively adapting shows humility, thoughtfulness and earns respect.

But don't let one person's doubt kill your drive. Filter the feedback. Keep what strengthens. Leave what weakens. You're still the captain of your 10% Project ship.

Circle Back and Say Thanks

After you've gathered feedback and made adjustments, don't forget to close the loop.

Tell people what you changed and thank them directly. A quick "Your feedback helped me see this differently" goes a long way.

Gratitude turns feedback into fuel. It also deepens support—people are way more likely to keep helping if they know their input mattered and was appreciated.

Expanding Your Reach

Want a secret weapon? Ask this simple question of everyone you talk to: "Is there someone else you think I should talk to about this?" It opens doors—fast. Your network grows exponentially.

The more feedback loops you create, the more resilient your idea becomes—and the more your credibility grows with each new connection.

Even if the project doesn't take off, the process *still pays off.* You've built trust, strengthened relationships, and shown initiative—those wins are real.

Don't underestimate the ripple effect. People will remember your thoughtfulness, hustle, and follow-up, long after your project ends.

Small Conversations Create Big Opportunities.

Start by asking two people for connections —
and watch how quickly your network (and your future) begins to expand.

One conversation.
Two introductions.
Endless possibilities.

Taking Feedback to the Next Level.

Engage with people who will be directly impacted by your project and do some user research. Understand their pain points and check that your proposed solution will address those pains. You might find some answers that surprise you and you will only improve your 10% Project. User research is a great way of identifying new possibilities or avoiding potential problems – both of which will make your 10% Project more powerful and will only add to the learning and value you gain from it.

CHAPTER 13

STEP 7: Jump into Action

This is the moment. Now it's time to take the leap—and bring your 10% Project into *reality*.

You've done the groundwork: brainstormed, defined your goal, shaped the idea, gathered insight, and refined your approach. You have a solid plan. Now comes the part that really separates dreamers from doers: taking action.

IMPLEMENT THE PLAN

Don't wait for perfect. Start with *progress*. The beauty of a 10% Project is that it's designed to teach you and evolve with you as you build it – step by step, hop by hop.

Why Implementation Matters

This is where intention becomes impact. All the preparation in the world doesn't mean much if it never leaves your head. You got your idea on paper... that's a big step, so now it becomes real.

Whether the outcome is a slam dunk or a quiet ripple, a soaring success or fabulous flop, the act of *doing* it shows courage, ownership, and grit. That's leadership in action.

You're proving that you don't just wait for opportunity—you *create* it. That mindset is what opens doors, builds confidence, and sparks lasting momentum.

Whenever you can, capture project milestones or metrics along the way that demonstrate the value or your efforts.

These are great to drop into updates, reviews and presentations about your progress.

Start Small, Stay Steady

No need to launch with fireworks. Start with one small step. One meeting. One draft. One pilot test.

Break the project into chunks and track progress like it's a video game—celebrate milestones and level-ups as you go.

Your first action might be scheduling a call, writing the intro, testing one version—whatever it is, do it. Every step builds muscle. Every win builds confidence.

Prepare for the Bumps

No plan survives first contact perfectly. Things will go sideways—delays, detours, dead ends. That's not failure. That's normal.

Use them as checkpoints, not stop signs. Pivot, reframe, try again. That's how real growth happens.

Each challenge is a test—and proof that you're becoming someone who can handle bigger and better things. That's the whole point.

Don't Forget: The Process *is* the Point

Even if your project doesn't become a runaway success, the experience still counts—massively.

Not every 10% Project explodes into a new career path or lands you in the spotlight right away. But every project teaches, stretches, and strengthens you. That *always* pays off.

Taking initiative *is* success. Building something from scratch, learning on the fly, growing your confidence—those are your core wins. Everything else is bonus.

Even if it fizzles out, people will remember that you tried. That you built something. That you *did something.* And next time? You'll be stronger, faster, and more focused.

The real win here is that you took initiative, demonstrated your problem-solving skills, and learned something new. You probably picked up some new skills, maybe had new experiences, and undoubtedly expanded your network. Even when projects don't succeed, they still position you as a proactive and capable leader.

Celebrate the Wins (All of Them)

No matter the outcome, celebrate. Seriously. You *started* something, *built* something, and *grew* through it. That's huge.

Think about what changed: Did you build new skills? Connect with people? Try something new? Stretch yourself in a way you're proud of? Honor those shifts. Let them sink in. This is how growth becomes identity. You're not the same person who started this project—and that's the point.

Share Your Journey

Don't keep your progress a secret. Post an update. Share a learning. Let others see you in motion. It builds credibility— and might inspire someone else.

Your early allies will feel proud to be part of your story—and they'll want to help you get across the finish line.

Plus, someone might have the missing piece, tool, or connection you need—but they won't know unless you *tell* them what you're working on.

And yes, share the mess too. It's relatable, human, and shows strength. Vulnerability builds trust. Trust builds momentum.

Let Them See What They Sparked

Real Talk

Remember Liz, the MBA student from Ohio State who first suggested that I write The 10% Project book?

I really wanted her to know the impact she had made — and what I had done with her suggestion.

So I reached out, let her know I had moved forward, and shared the progress I'd made.

Of course, this text led to a long catch-up phone call and plans to try and meet in person, despite being on opposite sides of the country.

You can see from her immediate response that Liz is definitely a keeper — when it comes to awesome friends, mentors, and all-around amazing people, keep them close!

Reflect, Learn, Evolve

When the dust settles, pause. Reflect. Capture what worked, what flopped, and what surprised you.

Write it down—yes, again! This becomes your blueprint for future projects. You're building not just one project, but a process you can repeat and grow.

Liz

Omg we have to talk when you have time... I am almost finished the 10% project book that you inspired me to do! And I am presenting the concept to a team at Adobe on the 20th!! Thank you for inspiring me!!

Thu, Apr 10 at 12:14 AM

Yes!!! Sunday and beyond will be great to catch up. I am graduating this Saturday so starting the last 3 days of classes!

This is all YOU! I am so excited you pursued it! The lives you could impact with this concept could be immense. Can't wait to hear all of the things! Hugs!

You'll build on your experiences, refining your approach with every new idea.

Keep it Rolling

Don't stop here. You've now unlocked a repeatable mindset— a system for growth, visibility, and meaning. Use it again. And again.

Maybe it's version 2.0 of your project—or maybe it's time for a totally new direction. Either way, you're not starting from scratch. You're starting *from experience.*

Stay curious. Stay brave. Keep building. One 10% Project at a time, you're changing how you work, lead, and live. That's legacy.

Dream > Do!

The difference between a "someday idea" and a real, career-shaping, life-lifting 10% Project? Action. That's it. Action makes everything else possible.

When you hit "go," you prove something powerful—not just to others, but to *yourself.* You're someone who doesn't wait. You *move.*

You're growing in real time. Gaining skills. Gaining clarity. And becoming the kind of person who shapes their future, you don't just wait for it to hopefully arrive.

The true ROI of a 10% Project isn't just the outcome—it's the confidence, the capacity, and the community you build in the process. That's what stays with you.

One project. Infinite future potential. Let this be the first of many. We have lots of tools to help you along the road. You've got this.

VISION BOARD

My 10% Project Name: _____

Networking

Mentoring

STEP 1:
Ignite
Your Spark

STEP 2:
Find Your
10% Project

STEP 3:
Own It.

The 10% PROJECT
Start Small. Dream Big.

Seven Simple
Steps

STEP 7:
Jump
Into Action

STEP 6:
Reflect
& Refine

STEP 5:
Share
the Vision

STEP 4:
Chart
the Course

Start Small. Dream Big.
Make it Happen.

My 10% Project Journey

Things always change... but let's set some goals.

Find your vision	Milestone 1	Milestone 2	Milestone 3	Milestone 4	Launch Date
_/_/_	_/_/_	_/_/_	_/_/_	_/_/_	_/_/_

CHAPTER 14

Why Write It Down?

So you've read all about the Steps 1 through 7. You totally get the concepts, you have a great idea, you're anxious to get started, and you're ready to launch – you can almost taste the satisfaction your 10% Project is going to give you.

You're excited, enthusiastic, you want to make it happen... so why spend that precious time just writing everything down when you could be making 'real progress'? You totally know what you're doing right? Maybe you're asking yourself, is Step 3 (the one about documenting your 10% Project) really that important?

The answer is a resounding **YES!**

I get it—writing stuff down sounds basic. Boring, even. But for your 10% Project... It's a power move. Not just helpful— *essential.* So essential it gets a whole chapter. Because writing is what turns vague dreams into real, buildable plans. It's the moment your idea steps out of the clouds and you confidently say, "Okay, let's do this."

Create a Solid Plan (That Stands Under Pressure)

Writing gives your ideas structure. You're not just scribbling— you're shaping. You're filling in blanks, noticing weak spots, and stress-testing your thinking before your idea is sent into the wild. It's like prepping your project with training wheels before you ride into traffic.

Writing slows you down—in the best way. It's your chance to pause and ask, "Does this make sense?" before charging full speed into a brick wall of confusion or complexity. When you write, you catch problems early and dodge them fast.

Make it Shareable (and Pitch-Ready)

Writing makes your idea shareable. Instead of mumbling something half-baked over coffee, you've got a clean, thoughtful version ready to send, share, present, or pitch.

A solid written version makes it easy for people to *get it*. They don't have to sit through a meeting—you can share a quick document or summary that they can read on the go. And once they understand it, they're more likely to support it.

A written idea is a living document. You can edit it, grow it, and crowdsource insights. Watch how quickly an initial idea sharpens up once it's passed around and stress-tested by other smart people.

When it's pitch time, you're not scrambling. Your idea is already organized, clear, and a few rounds better than when you started. Boom—you're ready.

Protect Your Genius (Seriously)

If you don't write it down, someone else might. Ideas get borrowed, rebranded, and launched by people who "heard something cool" and ran with it.

Maybe they heard you say it in a hallway or on a Zoom call. Fast forward—*they're* getting praise and visibility. You're left saying, "Wait, didn't I...?" Yes, yes you did. But if it's not written down, it didn't happen.

Write it down, and it's yours. Your name. Your thinking. Your timestamp.

Even if it never ships, it's still yours. Ownership matters. It shows you think strategically and invest in your ideas.

Keep a 10% Idea Vault

You're going to have a lot of ideas—some great, some wild, some half-baked. Capture them all. Make a folder or a document labeled "10% Vault" and drop ideas in as they come.

Even if you're not ready to act, your future you will thank you. One weird idea today could become your next breakout 10% Project six months from now.

Don't Underestimate What's in Your Brain

It's easy to dismiss your idea: "It's too small," "It's already been done," or "It's not ready."

Don't do it. Every idea has value.

Even "bad" ideas are teachers. They spark conversation, show you blind spots, or trigger better ideas. Share, listen, evolve. That's the magic loop.

So your project flops? That's OK. You just learned something others haven't. That's progress. That's fuel.

And sometimes that "meh" idea? It transforms into something brilliant when it meets the right brain or context.

Own Your Thinking

It's about pride. Documenting your ideas signals that you value your brain and its output, ideas, and innovation. That's powerful.

A written idea shows intent. It says, "I'm not just talking. I'm building." That's the first step toward visibility, traction, and opportunity.

Making It Real

Something happens when you see your ideas written down. There's something magical about seeing your thoughts on paper. Ideas that felt vague suddenly become concrete. You'll find yourself thinking, "Oh, this is actually doable!"

That confidence boost can be the difference between letting an idea fizzle out and actually making it happen.

Ideas click. Stop floating. Become real. Tangible. Doable.

And that moment of clarity? That's your launch fuel.
Suddenly, you believe in it. And that belief is often what turns a maybe into momentum.

Bottom line? Write it down. All of it. Even the weird stuff. Even the half-formed thoughts. Capture it before it disappears.

The world needs more of your ideas—*especially the brave, scrappy, "what if..." ones. So give them a chance to shine.*

"Working hard for something
we don't care about
is called stress;
Working hard for something
we love
is called passion."

Simon Sinek

SECTION 4
10% Projects Work for Anyone

CHAPTER 15

Who is The 10% Project for?

(Spoiler alert: Anyone who's ready to grow)

The beauty of The 10% Project is that it doesn't belong to one type of person.

It's not just for dreamers, doers, or disruptors.
It's for the curious. The restless. The stuck. The thriving.
The overwhelmed. The people on the edge of something —
even if they don't quite know what it is yet.

Because this framework doesn't require your life to be perfectly set up. It meets you where you are. And it grows with you.

The next few chapters break down how the 10% Project can be used in different seasons of life:

- For working professionals, it's a strategy for carving out impact, standing out, or falling back in love with their work.

- For job seekers, it's a way to rebuild confidence, craft direction, and regain momentum.

- For parents, it can be a tool to model intentional growth — or share a spark with your kids.

- For students, it's a chance to explore identity, passion, and purpose — get a head start in their career, without waiting for a diploma.

- For retirees, it's a way to rediscover meaning, leave a legacy, or simply stay lit up by life.

You don't have to read every chapter.
You don't need to relate to every group.
Think of this section like a sampler: pick the pieces that resonate and skip the ones that don't.
Or use it to understand how this framework could support the people around you.

Because growth isn't one-size-fits-all. The 10% Project was built to flex with your life — not demand you fit someone else's mold.

So whether you're building toward something new, recovering from something hard, or just ready for *more* — more momentum, more purpose, more joy — you'll find yourself somewhere in these pages.

It works because it's simple.
It sticks because it's personal.
And it's powerful because *you* make it your own.

Welcome to the part where the 10% Project starts meeting real life.

Your life.

Let's keep moving....

CHAPTER 16

10% Projects at Work

Be Great at Your Day Job (Your Cape Comes Later)

Before you launch your 10% Project, let's make one thing crystal clear: your boss needs to know you're crushing your core job. This isn't optional—it's the foundation. You have to do your day job really really well before you consider a 10% Project at work. Think of it like superhero mode: your regular role is Clark Kent. Your 10% Project is Superman. Both matter. One earns trust; the other builds legacy.

Dress for the job you want?

You've probably heard the advice: *"Dress for the job you want."*

It's well-meaning, but surface-level. Yes, presenting yourself professionally matters. But true career growth doesn't come from what you wear. It comes from what you *do.*

If you want to move toward your next opportunity, it's not just about looking the part— it's about *showing* you're already becoming it.

That's where a 10% Project can change everything. By intentionally choosing projects that build the skills, mindset, and experiences needed for your next role, you're creating visible proof of your readiness.

You're not waiting to be noticed. You're making it unmistakably clear you're ready. Because the real key isn't dressing up for the job you want, **it's stepping into the future you're building.**

Find Your Hidden Time (It's There—Promise)

Even the busiest pros have slivers of time they control. That hidden 10% isn't on your calendar—it's in the cracks. Between meetings. After emails. During that "mental checkout" lull.

The catch? No one admits to having free time at work. Why? Because that's how you end up with more meetings or someone asking, "Do we still need this role?" Keep it quiet, and use it wisely.

Even if your day feels jam-packed, look again. Free time hides in email scrolls, Slack wanderings, and five-minute buffers. Find it. Guard it. Use it.

How People Actually Use Their 10%

When people do have free time, they tend to fall into four camps:

- **Overachievers**
  They go all in on their core job. Their spreadsheets sparkle. Their inbox is empty. These folks double down on their current responsibilities, polishing their performance until it shines. They become the go-to expert for their tasks, which makes them almost irreplaceable. They become indispensable—but sometimes feel stuck.

- **Social Butterflies**
  Great at hallway chats and relationship-building. But too much talk, not enough traction.

  They spend the time chatting with colleagues. While networking can be useful, gossip or idle chatter rarely advances your career.

- **Clock Watchers**
  Tapped out. Drifting. Scrolling until 5:00. We've all been there. Just don't stay there. Frustrated and

feeling underappreciated, they check out mentally—scrolling through shopping sites or playing games, waiting for the day to end.

🌀 **Job Seekers**
Polishing résumés and refreshing LinkedIn.
They use this time to look for new opportunities, convinced that their skills will be better appreciated elsewhere. The goal... to get out. Valid—but what if you could build something amazing right where you are?

The 10% Power Play: Turn Spare Time into Spotlight

Instead of getting caught in these common traps, why not use that 10% of free time to kickstart a 10% Project that showcases your real potential? Whether it's solving a nagging problem at work, suggesting a process improvement, or designing a small innovation, it's all about being intentional with your time. Even a small idea can show initiative, creativity, and vision. That's career fuel.

Spot a broken process? A nagging inefficiency? Use your 10% Project to fix what others ignore. That's how reputations get made.

How to do a 10% Project Without Looking Like You're Just Not Busy Enough

Here are some ways to maximize that discretionary time without it looking like you haven't got enough 'real work':

🌀 **Start Small**
Identify a minor inefficiency or problem within your department. Draft a quick plan to address it. Don't launch a moonshot. Find a small pain point and brainstorm a fix. One doc, one diagram, one quick test. That's enough to start.

- **Loop In Your Manager (Early-ish)**
  Once it's taking shape, mention it to your boss—casually, confidently, and in the context of supporting the team. Mention it to your manager as something you're working on "in addition to your core duties."

- **Invite Allies**
  Share your thoughts with colleagues who might benefit from the project. Their input can help refine your approach. Share it with coworkers who'll get it. Collaborators help improve the idea—and build your internal fan club.

- **Show Results Fast**
  Aim for projects that can show visible progress within a few weeks. Small victories build momentum and credibility. Design your project for early wins. One improvement. One small shift. Get results people can see—and talk about.

What If Your Manager isn't into It?

Some managers aren't sold on side projects. That's okay. Your job is to make the case that it helps, not distracts.

Frame it as a tiny experiment to improve workflow, morale, or efficiency. Speak their language: results, not rebellion.

If they're still hesitant, no worries. Shift toward a project tied more directly to your current responsibilities. Prove your 9-to-5 is solid. Then circle back later.

Starter Ideas for 10% Wins at Work

- **Fix something broken**
  Simplify an outdated process.

- **Build a tool**
  Make a quick reference or how-to guide.

- **Process Improvements**
  Find a way to reduce repetitive tasks or streamline communication.

- **Learn something new**
  Level up your skills to help (or teach) your team.

- **Prototype a solution**
  Test a creative idea that saves time or money.

- **Skill Building**
  Use your free time to learn a new tool or develop a skill that benefits your team.

- **Team Support**
  Offer to organize something useful, like a quick reference guide or a shared resource library.

- **Creative Solutions**
  Experiment with small innovations that could save time or resources.

The Payoff: Visibility + Momentum

A well-executed 10% Project does two things: it boosts your reputation and makes your day job more interesting. You'll find that a small effort can lead to big changes—not just in your work, but in how people perceive your contribution. A small 10% Project can trigger big shifts— in culture and in how others see you. People notice value creators. Be one.

Make It Energizing, Not Exhausting

Your 10% Project shouldn't feel like homework. It should spark curiosity, joy, or a "What if?" question that won't leave you alone. If it energizes you, it'll show.

Choose wisely. Start small. Stay consistent. Let it evolve. You never know what doors your 10% Project might open—or who's watching. You never know where that extra 10% might take you!

How You're Perceived = Everything

Before you launch a 10% Project at work, remember this: perception is reality. Your core job needs to be solid—ideally, *exceptional*. Otherwise, your passion project might look like a shiny distraction.

Last thing you want is your manager or peer to be saying, "Wait... why are you building a new dashboard when your monthly report's still MIA?" Not a good look.

If your day job isn't dialed in, even the best side project will raise eyebrows—not praise.

First Things First - Excel at Your Core Responsibilities

Before going all in on a 10% Project, do a performance gut check. Are you delivering on the basics? Are you exceeding expectations? If not, start there.

A strong performance earns you permission to play with side projects. Show up, do great work, and you'll find support waiting when your big idea lands.

Self-Reflection

Think about the spectrum below:

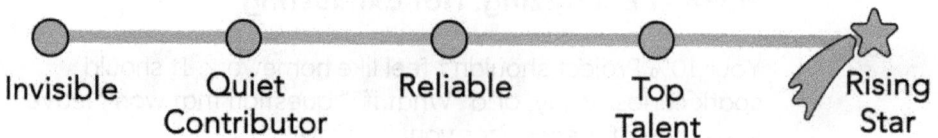

Invisible — Quiet Contributor — Reliable — Top Talent — Rising Star

Where would you place yourself today?

- Are you visible enough for the opportunities you want?
- Are you seen for your work — or are you quietly doing great things without the visibility or recognition you deserve?

This is exactly where a 10% Project makes all the difference. It's how you shift from invisible effort to visible impact.

If you want to move yourself closer to that 'Rising Star' zone, you don't need a giant leap. You just need one small, intentional step at a time — and that's exactly what a 10% Project helps you create.

Make Your Work Visible (Even the Invisible Parts)

Here's what many people don't realize - even as they work every day on doing the very best job they can: people often don't notice effort—they notice outcomes *and* visibility. You've got to show your work.

Recognition often follows visibility, not just results. The people getting credit? They're often the ones making their wins seen.

Sometimes, spending 5% less time doing and 5% more time sharing makes all the difference. Make your value tangible.

If your boss can't *see* your impact, it may as well not exist. It's your job to surface it—help them see the value you add and how well you are doing your job with tact and timing.

The same goes for missteps. Owning mistakes—and how you bounce back — builds more credibility than deflecting or just pretending they didn't happen.

Turn Mistakes into Momentum - Taking control.

A few years ago a good friend made a serious mistake. The kind that gets you a serious talking to from your manager. Initially he was angry, angry at himself, angry at his manager, angry at the world. But after we talked it through, instead of sulking, he flipped the script.

He reflected on what happened and how it happened, he owned it, and outlined a plan to fix it. More than that, he shared with his manager how he planned to take his lessons learned and teach his team proactively to avoid the same pitfall.

The result? His manager wasn't just relieved—she was impressed. The perception immediately shifted from careless to committed.

Mistakes are going to happen. What matters is the follow-through. Own it. Solve it. Share the lesson. That's leadership in action.

Own It, Fix It, Flip It

When something goes off-track, don't spiral. Get strategic. How can you turn this into an example of initiative and resilience? Made a mistake? Show how you think, how you fix it and make sure it never happens again. Had a misunderstanding? Clarify and reframe. Your response shapes the narrative.

Mistakes That Made Me

Mistakes aren't career-enders. They're often career *definers*— if you handle them right. Here are two moments I'll never forget. They didn't feel "teachable" at the time—but they really shaped how I lead, communicate, and recover.

No Film, Big Lesson

My first week in Public Relations. A major mayoral inauguration. My job? Capture the moment for the media.

I took every photo on a classic film camera (yes, this was back in the film days). I lined up beautiful shots. Felt proud. Then I walked into the darkroom, opened the back of the camera and realized...There was no film in it.

Panic! But, instead of spiraling, I took a breath and owned it. I reached out to a journalist I'd connected with that morning and explained what happened. I asked—genuinely—if he'd be willing to share a few of his photos for our communications.

He said yes without hesitation. That moment of humility created a relationship I leaned on for years. Even the mayor, who I told directly, respected the way I handled it.

Lesson? Own your error. Communicate clearly. And lead with the solution, not the panic.

Don't Quote me...
The Quote That Wasn't Approved

Fast forward years to a new job—first week again. This time: a major product launch.

I sent a pitch email to over 30 key journalists in the technology trade media. The press release? Perfect.

But the pitch email I used? It included a quote that hadn't been approved by a global electronics partner. Within hours, I got the dreaded email: **"This quote was never authorized. What happened?"**

I immediately took action:

- *Investigated the issue to discover exactly what happened*

- *Informed my boss—with the full timeline and action plan*

- *Sent a follow-up email to every journalist asking them not to use the quote*

- *Personally reached out to the outlet that had already published it asking them to update it with the approved version*

- *Wrote an apology to the customer*

Here's the twist: my boss actually thanked me for the way I handled the mistake. Not just for fixing it, but because it created a reason to reconnect with the customer—It showed we took our responsibilities seriously, were responsive and, in a way, actually ended up strengthening the relationship. I will never make that mistake again, but it wasn't the career killer I feared.

These moments taught me more about leadership, communication, and self-respect than any smooth success ever could.

I have never forgotten them – and never will. I'll also never make those mistakes again... ever. But I've shared these stories in job interviews, team meetings, and mentoring sessions for years.

Because people don't expect perfection. They want to see how you bounce back

What If You're Crushing It—and No One Notices?

It happens. You're delivering like a rockstar, but no one's clapping. Frustrating—but fixable.

Instead of simmering in resentment, shift gears: make it easier for people to notice. Visibility isn't bragging—it's part of the job.

Strategies to Be Seen Without Seeming Showy

1. **Share Updates Often**

    - Drop quick wins into your 1:1s or team Slack.
    - Keep it casual but consistent.
    - Be proactive in communicating your successes
    - Example: "Hey, just wanted to let you know we hit a milestone early—excited to keep it moving."

2. **Tie Your Wins to Team Goals**

    - Make it about "us," not just "me." Show how your work accelerates team momentum and adds value.
    - Example: "This report's early, which means the next team can start sooner." Framing matters.

3. **Keep a Win Journal**

    - Document your efforts like a pro. Not just for reviews—for *you*, too.
    - You can pull highlights into your next check-in, performance review, or LinkedIn update.
    - We've already discussed the advantages of documenting your 10% Project. Apply the same principle to your day-to-day work to ensure your contributions are recorded, seen, and recognized.

4. **Use Setbacks as Feedback**

    - There is always room for improvement, but sometimes it might feel like you're hitting wall after wall. Always look for a way to turn a negative into a positive.

- If the numbers are off, dig into the "why." Ask peers for input. Test a tweak.

- Show that you're engaged and iterating, not just hoping for better luck next quarter.

- If your role involves metrics you're struggling to meet (like sales targets), analyze why. Is it the product, the messaging, or your approach? If your colleagues are doing better, ask for their advice, and be open to trying new strategies.

- Consider how a 10% Project could help you learn something new that might change outcomes and show your commitment and persistence in your role. Who knows it might even help your entire team.

5. **Make Invisible Effort Visible**

- Show your process. Build a tracker. Share what you're testing.

- The story you tell about your effort matters. People respect progress, not just results.

- Creating a narrative around your effort can change the way your performance is perceived.

When Your 10% Project Is Crushing It... Quietly

If your side project is getting results but no buzz, try this:

Track + Share

- Keep a simple log of milestones you can pull into a team update or end-of-quarter review

Recruit Champions

- Bring in collaborators. Let them amplify the work.

- Bringing in colleagues to collaborate can increase visibility and give your project more credibility. When others see value, they'll naturally spread the word.

Map It to Team Wins

- "This project helps reduce X. That saves time across the team." Instant relevance.
- Make it clear how your project aligns with broader objectives: "This initiative could help streamline our workflow, saving time across the team."

Mentors + Networks: Your Secret Career Jetpack

When it comes to launching a 10% Project inside your workplace, nothing accelerates progress quite like mentorship and networking. These two elements aren't just helpful—they're game-changers.

Mentors help you think bigger, avoid mistakes, and communicate your ideas clearly. Networks expand your reach—getting your project seen, supported, and shaped by collaborators who care.

A coffee chat might unlock a resource you didn't know existed. A peer's feedback could sharpen your pitch before you take it to your boss. These small moments of connection? They stack up.

A solid mentor can help you spot landmines, refine your pitch, and navigate organizational politics with ease. And your network? It can amplify your idea faster than you could alone, getting it in front of the right people at the right time. A conversation over coffee might lead to a key introduction. A quick Slack message might spark a collaborator. This is how momentum builds.

In fact, networking and mentoring are *so* important, they deserve entire chapters of their own (don't worry—we've got you covered in the pages ahead). But here's a preview: if your 10% Project is the spark, your mentor and network are the kindling that turns it into a bonfire.

Want your 10% Project to provide a real career lift? Don't go it alone. Pull in support, learn from others, and surround yourself with people who see what you're trying to build—and want to help you build it faster.

Balance = Credibility + Curiosity

To make your 10% Project fly, your day job needs to shine. That's your credibility card. Play it well.

Strong performance opens the door for creativity. People don't worry about side quests when the main mission is handled.

And if no one's noticing? Speak up. Strategically. Consistently. Give your work the spotlight it deserves.

The best 10% Projects don't just add flavor to your role—they enhance it. They solve real problems, spark new energy, and sometimes even rewrite how people see your potential.

Remember: the best 10% Projects make your whole job more rewarding. That's the win. That's the future.

CHAPTER 17

Creating 10% Projects at Home

(Without Breaking Your Chill)

Finding Your Rhythm: Relaxation + Growth

Home is your haven. It's where you drop the workday armor, binge-watch guilt-free, and ideally breathe without a to-do list chasing you down. Whether you're juggling a full-time job, managing a household, balancing school, or just trying to find time to breathe, you deserve downtime. You *need* that space. You *deserve* that space.

But what if a sliver of intentional effort—just 10%—made your whole home life feel more joyful, meaningful, or energizing?

The Rut Trap

Relaxing is essential. But endless scrolling or binge-watching episodes can eventually blur together. You're *resting*—but can also get kind of... stuck. It's easy to fall into the comfort of routinely watching your favorite series or scrolling through social media. It is undeniably relaxing, but after a while, it can feel like you're just passing time instead of truly enjoying it.

On the flip side, launching a home project can feel like one more thing. Especially if the people you live with are more "Why are we doing this?" than "Let's go!"

The win? Balance. Protect your rest *and* give yourself a sliver of time to explore something fun, weird, creative, or personally satisfying. That's the sweet spot—and where your 10% Project lives.

How to Find Your 10% at Home - Where the Time Hides

Even at home, there are little time pockets hiding in plain sight. Find them, claim them, and gently redirect them toward something that sparks your brain.

Think: 30 minutes before the house wakes up. That post-dinner calm. A Saturday morning slice. You don't need hours—just enough to begin.

Here are a few sneaky-smart ways to make space for your home-based 10% Project:

- **Morning Minutes**
  Wake up 10 minutes earlier. Set your alarm just 10 minutes earlier and dedicate that time to brainstorming or planning your project. Use it to sketch, journal, plan, or simply to *dream*.

- **Screen Swap**
  One less episode = one more step forward on your idea. Netflix won't mind. Swap one episode of your show for a half-hour of creative time. (You can always watch it later!)

- **Family Collaboration**
  Get your family involved. Make your project something everyone can contribute to— Pull in your crew. Create a garden. Issue a cooking challenge. Start a goofy podcast. Your 10% Project becomes play for friends and family and then the world.

- **Weekend Window**
  Set aside a fixed time each weekend just for your project—no chores, no errands, just you & your ideas.

Typing in the Dark: The Sound of Commitment

Some of the most meaningful time I've made for my 10% Projects hasn't looked glamorous at all. It's looked like me, sitting at the desk under my daughter's loft bed at night, quietly typing while she drifts off to sleep.

I used to worry that she'd be annoyed by the sound — the soft clack of keys in the dark. But instead, she told me once, "I like hearing it. It helps me fall asleep." Because to her, it's the sound of commitment. The sound of focus. The sound of her mum showing up for something that matters — night after night.

She's learning that dreams don't wait for perfect timing. That sometimes, we make progress in small moments, stolen from the edges of the day. And that doing something for yourself isn't selfish — it's modeling something powerful.

So if you're squeezing your 10% Project into late-night hours or early-morning silence... know that it counts.
And someone might just be learning from the quiet rhythm of your determination.

Home-Based 10% Project Ideas

- **Creative Pursuits**
  Write that book you've been dreaming of *(you're reading mine right now)*, start a personal blog, or learn an instrument.

- **Fix & Flourish**
  Organize one thing. Make a cozy corner. DIY something small.

- **Level-Up Time**
  Develop a new skill like painting, gardening, or photography and use it to connect to people with the same passions. Learn a language or a new skill through an online course.

- **Give Back**
  Volunteer for a local cause, plan a neighborhood event, or start a community newsletter. Be the glue and expand your networking in new and amazing ways... 10% Projects like this can help so many people and unlock incredible and unforeseen opportunities for you at the same time.

Dealing with Family Critique

Not everyone will understand why you're suddenly interested in pottery or writing poetry in the evenings. Family members might raise an eyebrow or wonder why you're not just kicking back. The key is communication—let them know why your 10% Project matters to you. Share your enthusiasm and invite them to be part of it if they're interested.

The Benefits of a Home 10% Project

- **Mental Refresh**
  Engaging your brain differently can bring more interest to your life, making you more fulfilled and happier.

- **Skill Building**
  You might discover a talent you never knew you had.

- **Personal Satisfaction**
  Completing a small project gives you a sense of accomplishment.

- **Family Bonding**
  Working on something together can strengthen connections and create lasting memories.

A 10% Project at home that gives me joy every day

Jumping into 10% at Home: The Topiary Kangaroo

Last summer, I decided I wanted a six-foot topiary kangaroo for my garden. Turns out, no one really makes them. And the other types of topiary animals that do exist – deer, elephants, teddy bears? Ridiculously expensive!

So I did what any 10% Project enthusiast might do: I decided to make one myself.

I spent my weekends researching plant types, making return trips to the hardware store, and trial-and-erroring my way through frame construction. My 10-year-old daughter helped me shape and plant it—then asked for a joey-sized one of her own. So of course... we built two.

We laughed. We learned. We made mistakes (a few plants didn't make it). And now? Every morning, I walk past our topiary kangaroos and smile. It's become a neighborhood landmark. It's also become a quiet ritual—a little reminder of what's possible when you follow an idea, however weird, and give it a little time and care.

The best part? It keeps growing. Year after year, with just a little shaping and nurturing, it becomes more beautiful and more us. Just like the best 10% Projects do.

Making It Sustainable

Your home 10% Project shouldn't feel like a chore. Keep it light, keep it fun, and adjust if it starts feeling stressful. The goal is to enhance your personal life, not turn your free time into a second job.

Stay Curious

Whether it's a small creative outlet or a practical improvement, a 10% Project at home is all about making your personal space more enjoyable. Take that little step towards something you've always wanted to try. You might just find that adding a pinch of creativity to your routine makes relaxation even more satisfying.

CHAPTER 18

Finding or Designing Your Next Job

Stuck, Between Jobs, or Starting Over? Start Here. Use Your 10% Project to Find (or Design) Your Next Job

If you're job-hunting, burnt out, or trying to return after a long break—it's normal to feel discouraged. Confidence dips. Direction gets fuzzy. And the job search grind? It's brutal.

It's hard to feel hopeful when even figuring out what you *want* feels like a puzzle. But there's a powerful, low-pressure way to rebuild momentum: a 10% Project.

With just a sliver of time and energy, you can try something new, rebuild your skills, and make connections that might open real doors. All without staring at another blank job application form.

In the real world, most jobs never get posted publicly. According to LinkedIn, up to **85% of jobs are filled through networking**, not traditional applications. That means building genuine relationships and showing what you can do—*before* the job exists—is your biggest competitive edge. A 10% Project gives you something real to talk about, share, and connect around. It turns you from a résumé into a person with momentum.

Why a 10% Project Works When Everything Else Feels Broken

Think you need a polished résumé or a big vision to make progress? You don't. A 10% Project starts where you are, with what you've got—and helps you build forward. It's small, personal, energizing... and zero pressure.

All you need is curiosity and the courage to start *something*. That one small thing? It could shift everything.

Rebuild Your Confidence—One Tiny Project at a Time

If you've been out of the game for a while, it's easy to start losing confidence —wondering if you've still got it? You do. But you might need proof—and a 10% Project gives you that.

When you make something—anything—you shift from waiting to creating. You build your own power and direction.

A 10% Project helps break that cycle of self-doubt by giving you something tangible to work on—something that proves how much you have to offer.

- **Start Small**
  One idea. One weekend. One coffee-fueled brainstorm.

  Don't overthink it. Pick something that genuinely interests you—maybe volunteering for a local cause, organizing a community event, or building a portfolio project from home.

- **Rebuild Skills**
  Dust off an old strength—or dip your toes into something totally new. Choose a 10% Project that lets you practice something you used to be good at or something new you've always wanted to try. It doesn't have to be perfect; it just has to get you moving - one step at a time.

- **Track the Wins**
  Even tiny victories count. Set up a "Wins" doc. Screenshot the progress. Print the email. Build your momentum.

Feeling Trapped in a Job that just isn't you? Start Building the Exit.

If your job is draining your soul, your 10% Project becomes your oxygen mask. It's your creative outlet—and your escape tunnel. A 10% Project can become your life vest. It's a way to explore something you love without risking your paycheck.

You don't need to quit to start fresh. Your 10% Project builds new skills, connections, and confidence on the side.

Plus, it's a reason to look forward to Monday again and you never know… perhaps as you change, your current job might change along with you and become a job that actually fits.

- **Build Strategic Skills**
  Choose something your dream job would love to see on your résumé. Bonus if it's fun, too. Use your 10% Project to gain skills that might help you transition to a new role—like learning a new software or honing your leadership abilities.

- **Create What You Crave**
  If your day job is uninspiring, your 10% Project can reignite your passion. If your current job feels like it is sucking the life out of you, your 10% Project can bring back the spark.

- **Build a Better Network**
  When you work on something you care about, the right people show up. Let them in. Your 10% Project can naturally connect you with people who share your interests, building new networks and leading to new opportunities.

A 10% Project acts as a bridge, giving you something current to talk about and showing that you're proactive about personal growth.

It shows you're *already* growing, learning, contributing. No awkward gaps—just forward motion.

- **Refresh + Relearn**
  Pick a project that refreshes your skills or introduces new ones. Take a course. Start a blog. Build a small website. Your future employer will be impressed. Taking an online course and documenting your learning journey is a great way to demonstrate commitment.

- **Get seen**
  Share updates, reflect on your learnings, post milestones. This isn't bragging—it's building your personal brand. Share your progress on social media, connect with groups related to your project, and let your enthusiasm be your calling card.

- **Create Proof**
  Use your project to create something tangible—a report, a small website, a video series—anything that shows your skills in action. Build a portfolio that says, "I'm not waiting—I'm building." Even a simple project speaks volumes.

10% Project Ideas to Reboot Your Career

- **Personal Branding**
  Build a blog, or LinkedIn series on your industry. Create a website to share your ideas and showcase your expertise.

- **Freelance Experiment**
  Take on a small gig that aligns with your skills and interests. Find a short gig on Fiverr, Upwork, or offer

your time to a local nonprofit.

- ⊜ **Learning Challenge**
  Dedicate time to mastering a tool or skill you've always wanted to learn. Try a 30-day challenge: 30 Canva designs, 30 posts, 30 lines of code.

- ⊜ **Community Engagement**
  Organize a local workshop or a digital event to connect with like-minded people.

- ⊜ **Passion Pursuit**
  Start that creative project you've been putting off—it might just lead to something bigger. Record that podcast. Write the first chapter. Publish one post. Start.

Keeping Yourself Going

Motivation dips are normal. That's why joy and celebrating small wins really matters. Make it something you *look forward to*. That's the secret.

Break it into mini-goals. Celebrate them. Light candles. Bake cookies. Rewards matter.

Progress is progress. Even on the messy days. Especially then.

Your Comeback Starts Here

A 10% Project can be your comeback story. It's about proving to yourself that you're capable, resilient, and worthy of new opportunities.

This isn't about a résumé. It's about your confidence, your creativity, your momentum.

A 10% Project reminds you that you've still got it. You've *always* had it.

Whether it's landing a new job, rediscovering your passion, or simply feeling proud of what you've accomplished, your project will remind you that you're still moving forward —this work *matters*. It will shine through in your next interview and show the hiring manager you are someone they need on their team.

Dream Big, Start Small

You don't need to have it all figured out. You just need to begin.

Stay curious. Follow your energy. Let your 10% Project take you somewhere unexpected.

One day, your 10% Project might just turn into your next job, your next chapter... or your next big leap. The most important thing? Believe that you're still in the game—because you are...

CHAPTER 19

The College 10% Project Advantage

Get Noticed Before You Graduate

Stepping Ahead Before the Ink Dries on Your Diploma

You've spent four (or more) years grinding through classes, group projects, ramen-fueled finals, and maybe a few life-altering coffee habits. Then comes graduation. Diploma in hand. The world awaits.

But here's the twist—so does everyone else. Same degree. Same GPA. Same bullet points on a résumé. And suddenly, the job hunt feels like trying to get noticed at a concert where *everyone* is yelling.

So how do you stand out?

Easy: Do something extra. Something real. Something that shows who you are, not just what you've studied. That's what a 10% Project is for.

Students who add 10% Projects to their college experience, graduate with more than a degree—they leave with *momentum*.

They've tested skills, built portfolios, networked early, and maybe even scored offers, all before tossing their cap in the air.

Balancing Dorm Life + Dream Jobs

No one's saying skip the parties. College is about fun, growth, late-night debates, and probably some midnight snacks.

But you can live fully *and* plan smart. A 10% Project is the secret weapon that lets you do both.

While others are still "figuring it out," you'll already have something real to talk about—something that makes you impossible to ignore.

What Employers Actually Want

Degrees matter. But employers want more. They want proof of initiative, creativity, and results. A 10% Project screams all three.

Want to get hired? Be the student who did more than just passed all their classes—be the one who *built* something real.

Employers love graduates who come prepared with more than just theoretical knowledge. They want problem-solvers, self-starters, and people who've proven they can take initiative. That's exactly what a 10% Project showcases.

- **Actions speak louder than words – and amplifies the words on your diploma**
  Instead of just listing your degree on your resume, you can showcase actual 10% Projects—like leading a student group, creating a community initiative, or launching a small side business. Show real-world results, not just classroom content.

- **Build Your Network Now**
  While your classmates are just starting to figure out their next steps, you'll already have connections in your desired field. Professors, event speakers, collaborators—you're not just making friends, you're planting career seeds.

- **Lead with Passion**
  Choose a 10% Project that aligns with your career goals and demonstrates commitment and enthusiasm—qualities that make employers take notice. Projects aligned with your major = clarity, purpose, and a huge résumé boost.

Where to Start: Easy Wins with Big Career Payoffs

- **Professional Passion**
  Start a blog or YouTube channel about a topic related to your major. Share insights, reviews, or tutorials. It shows you're engaged in the field beyond your coursework. Create content around your major, like Finance tips for Gen Z, design tutorials, science explainers.

- **Volunteer in Your Field**
  Offer your skills to a non-profit or community group. Whether it's social media management, tutoring, or event planning, it's hands-on experience. Offer your skills to real organizations: manage their social media, write for their blog, organize events.

- **Campus Innovation**
  Build what's missing on campus. A creative showcase. A business pitch night. A student-run service. Create a club or organize an event that aligns with your interests. For example, a coding hackathon if you're a computer science major or a debate series for political science students.

- **Collaborative Learning**
  Team up with classmates to tackle a real-world problem. Propose a sustainability project on campus or develop an app prototype as a group. Solve a problem. Build something. Share it. Then put it in your portfolio

Keep It Manageable—But Moving

Midterms will hit. Deadlines will pile up. That's okay. Your 10% Project isn't another class—**it's a playground**. Keep showing up for it in small ways.

The goal isn't perfection. It's progress. Show up imperfectly. Show up late. Just show up.

How to Make It Interview Gold

Your 10% Project isn't filler. It's your *lead story*. Put it at the top of your résumé. Showcase results, ownership, and impact.

Did you grow engagement by 25%? Launch a website? Coordinate volunteers? Name it. Numbers win interviews.

Focus on outcomes. Don't just describe it—*quantify it*. Showing tangible results will make all the difference.

Tell Your Project Story Like a Pro

Structured interviews—the kind that ask, *"Tell me about a time when..."*—are used by **over 90% of Fortune 500 companies** to evaluate candidates. That means storytelling isn't optional—it's how you stand out. That's exactly where your 10% Project shines.

So next time they ask, *"Tell me about a time you took initiative,"* you won't fumble for an answer. You'll confidently share your 10% Project story, demonstrating your proactive mindset, creative problem-solving, and willingness to grow.

Employers love candidates who don't just follow the script— they write their own.

You've got a real story. Practice it. Own it. Deliver it. The confidence you gain from doing the work? That's what sets you apart. Be the person who writes their own career plot twist. That's who they hire.

Highflying Lady Bugs: Passion Beats Paper

At Boeing, I once sorted through hundreds of resumes to hire a digital content creator. Degrees? Check. Certifications? Check. Endless buzzwords? Check.

But Michael stood out.

Not because of his degree — Telecommunications, which honestly sounded more like "phone systems" than marketing — but because of the four years he spent running his own startup, Ladybug Media Group.

- *He had real-world experience:*
- *Marketing*
- *Content*
- *Video production*
- *Digital strategy*
- *Design*

Talking to him, his passion was unmistakable. He didn't just know the theory. He lived the work. That's why I brought him to Silicon Valley. That's why he landed the job — and at a higher salary than he expected.

Michael didn't call it a 10% Project. But he lived the spirit of one long before it had a name. And that side project? It launched him into his dream career in aerospace.

Why It Matters Way Beyond College

This isn't just about your first job—it's about building a career that keeps evolving *with* you.

If you keep flexing your 10% mindset throughout your career. You won't just have a degree—you'll have experience, connections, and stories that set you apart.

You'll be the one who grows faster, who gets noticed, promoted, and remembered, gets picked first, and creates their own opportunities for years to come.

Have Fun. Stay Curious. Do One Thing.

You don't need to choose between late-night pizza and building your future. You don't need to give up fun to get ahead—you just need to be a little intentional with a fraction of your spare time... 10%.

Start small. Stay curious. Follow that idea that keeps tapping you on the shoulder. It could change everything.

Let your 10% Project be the thing that makes your college experience even more rewarding. When graduation day comes, you'll be more than just prepared—you won't just be ready for the job market. You'll already be in motion.

CHAPTER 20

Start Early: Helping Kids Build the 10% Mindset

Start Them Young. Watch Them Soar.

Imagine this: a child who's confident, curious, and not afraid to try something new. Who sees a problem and says, "I can fix that." That's the power of starting the 10% mindset early.

The good news? You don't have to wait until adulthood to start building this kind of resilient proactive mindset. 10% Projects are just as powerful for kids—and can shape how they see themselves forever.

Whether it's a lemonade stand, a craft table, or a podcast with their best friend—these projects aren't just fun. They build real skills, real confidence, and real momentum.

Why It's Worth Starting Now

Kids aren't thinking about careers—yet. But they are forming the habits and attitudes that will define how they tackle life. This is where it all begins. Teaching kids to plan, tinker, create, and follow through, gives them something priceless: belief in their own abilities.

They are soaking up habits and attitudes that will shape their futures. Teaching them how to think critically, plan projects, and see things through, not only boosts their confidence, but also sets the foundation for future success.

- **Real-Life Skills**
  Planning, organizing, communicating, and problem-solving become second nature. From organizing materials, to talking to adults—they're learning by doing.

- **Independent Thinking**
  Kids learn to take ownership of their ideas and see how effort leads to results. *"I made this happen"* becomes part of how they see themselves.

- **Grit in Action**
  When it doesn't go perfectly? That's where the real learning kicks in. Not every project will succeed, but the experience teaches resilience and persistence. Teach them critical lessons early and they'll reap the benefits for life.

Let's Get Creative: Kid-Friendly 10% Ideas

- **The Classic Lemonade Stand**
  Teach basic business skills like marketing, pricing, money handling, and customer service with a smile. Even skills like manufacturing (the best lemonade on the street), making sure supplies are on hand, and cultivating patience to wait for customers to walk by.

- **Craft Pop-Ups**
  Create and sell friendship bracelets, bookmarks, or keychains at events. Making and selling crafts at school events.

- **Book Review Blog**
  Encouraging reading and critical thinking by sharing their favorite books. Builds writing skills and confidence in their opinions.

- **Neighborhood Helper Service**
  Offer pet-sitting, lawn care, or small chores—earning a bit of pocket money while learning responsibility.

◖ **Young Entrepreneurs**
Help them set up a small online store selling handmade items or arts and crafts – with parental supervision.

Real-Life Success Stories: Real Kid Projects That Grew Up Big

Want some inspiration for you or your kids?

◖ **Moziah Bridges -** fashion brand (& was even seen on Shark Tank). At just 9 years old, Moziah started his bow tie business, Mo's Bows, which grew into a booming fashion brand.

◖ **Alina Morse -** Zollipops now sell in Target and Kroger. At age 7, Alina created sugar-free lollipops. She founded Zollipops, and her products are now sold nationwide.

◖ **Mikaila Ulmer -** Me & the Bees Lemonade. Inspired by her love of bees and a family recipe Mikaila at just 4 years old (and presumably with really supportive parents), launched lemonade with a bee-saving mission. Today, "Me & the Bees" is stocked in major grocery stores nationwide.

These are incredible success stories, but remember it is the journey and the lessons that your kids learn which are the main thing, no matter how a project turns out. Remember, start small but always dream big.

Parenting the Project (Without Taking It Over)

While kids are bursting with ideas, they'll need some guidance and support.

Kids have wild ideas—they just need structure and support. The trick is to let them take the lead, while offering help when needed. Guide without doing.

- **Co-Create the Idea**
  Encourage them to come up with ideas they're genuinely excited about. Brainstorm. Ask questions. But let *them* decide what excites them.

- **Goal Setting**
  Help them set small, achievable goals so they see progress. First goal: make one flyer, sell one cookie, write one post.

- **Encourage Problem Solving**
  Resist the urge to fix everything for them—guide them to figure it out. If it breaks or flops, ask: "What could we try next?"

- **Cheer Them On**
  Celebrate their efforts, not just the outcomes. It's about building confidence, not just success. Reward the try, the tweak, the bounce-back. That's the win.

Skills That Stick for Life

- **Planning and Organization**
  Turning a vague idea into a structured project. Project planning = mental muscle for life.

- **Communication Skills**
  Talking to adults, pitching ideas, and building confidence. Speaking up builds social intelligence and confidence.

- **Financial Literacy**
  Those small projects like selling crafts teach basic budgeting. Even $5 in profits teaches value and decision-making.

- **Resilience**
  Learning to bounce back from setbacks builds character. Learning from "oops" moments makes them stronger humans.

From Backyard Hustles to Life Readiness - From Fun to Future Skills

You don't need a future mogul. Just a kid who sees their ideas as *possible.*

The goal is mindset: "I can make something happen." because that confidence will grow with them.

As they grow, the mindset of looking for opportunities, taking small risks, and being creative will serve them well in every aspect of life.

They'll learn to experiment, create, and bounce back. Those are life's ultimate success skills.

Grow Bold Kids

When we teach kids that their ideas matter, we plant something powerful. Confidence. Creativity. Courage.

Let them try. Let them mess up. Let them shine. That's where leadership begins.

Whether they build a business or just build belief in themselves, it's a win.

And hey—one of those "just for fun" ideas? It might be the thing they talk about in their TED talk someday.

CHAPTER 21

10% Projects in Retirement

Purpose, Connection, and Joy

Finding What's Next (When you can finally Ignore the Alarm Clock)

Retirement: the reward after decades of hustle. No more commutes. No more late meetings. Just freedom… and maybe a quiet moment thinking, "Now what?"

The truth? Once the "honeymoon phase" fades, many retirees feel a little unanchored. No more routine. No more team. No more clear purpose.

It's not uncommon to feel a little lost without the rhythm of work life.

That's where a 10% Project comes in—something small, meaningful, flexible. A way to bring your experience forward *without* committing to a second career – unless of course you want to.

Why It's Harder Than It Looks

Statistics don't lie: many retirees feel a real loss of purpose.

Studies show that retirees often experience a sense of loss— loss of identity, purpose, and routine. According to the American Psychological Association, about 30% of retirees struggle with finding meaning in their post-work lives, and some experience increased feelings of loneliness or depression.

Add to that a drop in daily social interactions and structure, and it's no surprise that some retirees experience dips in mood, motivation, and mental sharpness.

But it doesn't have to stay that way. Retirement can be a launchpad—a fresh chapter where you explore interests, reconnect with purpose, and maybe do the thing you never had time for when you worked five days a week.

It can create the time and opportunity to explore new interests, reconnect with the community, or even embark on a passion project that was previously on the back burner.

And because it's small and self-directed, a 10% Project gives just the right nudge to stay sharp, creative, and connected.

A 10% Project is perfect for retirees because it's flexible, personal, and just the right size to keep you motivated without feeling overwhelmed.

Your Next Chapter Isn't the End—It's the Upgrade

You didn't retire *from* something—you retired *into* something.

You've built wisdom and perspective that the world still needs. You have decades of experience, knowledge, and skills just waiting to be applied in new, exciting ways. The question is: where do you want to apply them now?

10% Projects help bridge that gap between rest and purpose. They bring structure, joy, and progress—without the burnout.

A 10% Project is a fantastic way for retirees to re-engage with life, make use of their hard-earned skills, and pursue passions without the pressure of a full-time commitment. It's an opportunity to build a fulfilling routine that balances activity with the relaxation you've work so hard to earn.

Stay Connected, Stay Sharp

Without the daily rhythm of work, it's easy to slip into isolation. That's why 10% Projects work—they invite you back into conversation, creation, and contribution.

Whether it's mentoring, volunteering, or learning a new skill, 10% Projects keep your calendar—and your brain—engaged.

People who stay mentally and socially active in retirement live longer, report higher happiness, and feel more fulfilled. That's no coincidence.

Retirement 10% Project Ideas- Give Back or Get Involved

Here are some ideas to get started with a 10% Project in retirement:

- **Mentoring Programs**
  Share your career wisdom with younger professionals.

- **Local Volunteering**
  Help at community gardens, libraries, or charity shops.

- **Teaching a Skill**
  Host workshops or classes on crafts, cooking, or professional skills.

Turn Experience into Expression

- **Start a Small Business**
  Turn a hobby into a side hustle—like selling crafts online.

- **Public Speaking**
  Offer talks at community centers or schools on your area of expertise or passion.

- ⚫ **Write your story**
  Share your career journey, a personal passion, or create a memoir, a blog or a podcast.

- ⚫ **Become a consultant**
  Freelance or consult part-time. Offer your professional skills on a flexible, part-time basis.

Personal Growth and Leisure

- ⚫ **Start a 10% Project that aligns with your passions**
  Learn to play a musical instrument or master a new language and in the process make a new circle of friends.

- ⚫ **Document Family History**
  Create a digital archive or write a family history to share with your extended family.

- ⚫ **Try Something Just For You**
  Whether it's a book club or a hiking group, learning a new language, or mastering an instrument, staying engaged socially matters.

The Social Multiplier Effect

Research indicates that staying socially active in retirement is crucial to maintaining both mental and physical health. A study published in the Journal of Aging and Health found that retirees who engage in social and community activities report higher levels of well-being and longevity.

Social engagement = better health. It's science. From community projects to shared hobbies, staying connected keeps you sharper and happier.

Taking on a 10% Project can help maintain this vital social connection— And the best part? These projects create relationships—just by doing what you love.

Keep It Going—Without Burning Out

Even the best projects hit a lull. Here's how to keep it fun and sustainable:

- ● **Break It Down**
  Set micro-goals that feel energizing, not exhausting. Set small, manageable goals. Maybe it's attending one community event a month or spending a couple of hours each week on a passion project.

- ● **Celebrate Progress**
  Even small achievements deserve recognition. Mark your progress with little rewards or share your achievements with friends and family. Celebrate. Even the tiny wins. Especially those.

- ● **Stay Curious**
  Surprise yourself. Try something weird. That's where joy often hides. Explore new interests, even if they're outside your comfort zone. Sometimes the best projects are the ones that surprise you.

A Little Extra, If You Want It

Want your 10% Project to bring in a little cash? Great. As long as it stays joyful, go for it.

Whether it's travel, treats, or grandkid gifts—a little income can add sparkle to your lifestyle.

Think about it this way: you spent decades building skills and gaining expertise—why not leverage that knowledge in a way that's both enjoyable and profitable? The beauty of a 10% Project is that it doesn't have to feel like a "job." Instead, it's an opportunity to explore something you love while also earning a little on the side.

The key is this: if it feels like a job, pause. If it feels like play with the bonus of a paycheck? Lean in.

Protect Your Peace!

It's easy to accidentally fall into the trap of working as hard in retirement as you did during your career. The freedom to take on new projects can sometimes lead to overcommitting. A 10% Project helps set clear boundaries, allowing you to stay productive without losing the sense of freedom you've worked so hard to achieve.

Remember, the goal is to stay active and engaged while also enjoying the flexibility of retirement. It's about finding the sweet spot between contributing meaningfully and savoring your well-deserved downtime.

You earned this time. A 10% Project should *add* to your life, not consume it. Boundaries matter.

Let your 10% Project be your *favorite part of the day,* not your new full-time gig.

Thrive on Your Terms

This chapter of life is yours. What do you want to explore? Create? Give? Share?

A 10% Project is your permission slip to *start small,* stay curious, and keep moving forward.

The goal isn't productivity—it's purpose. The kind that makes you smile, stretch, and say, "I did that."

Retirement is your time to thrive on your terms. There's no boss, no deadlines—just you and the endless possibilities ahead. A 10% Project can help you stay engaged, connect with others, and continue to grow. Embrace this new phase with curiosity, humor, and the confidence that your best projects are still ahead of you.

You've earned the freedom. Now go use it however *you* want. The best is still very much ahead.

"Life is either
a daring adventure
or nothing at all."

Helen Keller

SECTION 5
Making the most of
Opportunities

CHAPTER 22

Building Your Personal Brand with a 10% Project

You Are Your Own Brand

Most people don't walk around thinking, "I am a brand." But the truth is—you are. Your words, your actions, your projects, your follow-through—it's all shaping how people experience, see, and perceive you. And that perception? It either draws opportunity to you or lets it pass by.

That's where your 10% Project becomes a personal branding super tool. It gives you a concrete, story-worthy, *visible* way to show up, show who you are and what you stand for.

Brand Identity vs. Reputation: The Alignment Game

- **Your Brand Identity** is how you *want* to be known: "curious", "creative", "strategic", "dependable".
- **Your Reputation** is how others *actually* describe you when you're not in the room.

A 10% Project helps you bring those two into alignment. It becomes your proof point. Instead of just saying, "I'm innovative," you can show a project where you *were*.

Try this:

Ask three people who know you well, "What's one word you'd use to describe me professionally?"

Their answers = a glimpse into your current brand.

Perception Is Power

Perception is often a more significant factor in success than pure talent or hard work. If people perceive you as disengaged, stuck in a rut, or uninspired, they might overlook your potential—even if you're quietly doing a great job.

You could be a top performer behind the scenes—but if no one sees it, it's like whispering into a void.

A well-framed 10% Project helps *make the invisible visible*.

If they see you as motivated, creative, and eager to take on new challenges, they're more likely to involve you in exciting projects, promotions, or opportunities.

That's where a 10% Project comes in. It's not just about what you do—it's about how others see what you do. A well-chosen project shines a light on your best qualities: your initiative, your curiosity, your willingness to make things happen. This kind of perception can completely shift how you're seen by colleagues, managers, mentors, and even new contacts.

When people see you taking initiative, solving problems, and showing creative leadership—even in small ways—it shifts how they talk about you and what doors they open for you.

Your Online Presence: Digital Brand = Real Impact

Whether or not you're actively "building a brand" online, your digital trail is doing it for you. A 10% Project gives you something real and authentic to share:

- A lesson you learned
- A behind-the-scenes peek
- A "how it started vs. how it's going"

You don't need to post every day. Just *share your process* in a way that feels natural. Even a quick update on LinkedIn, in a Slack channel, or a team newsletter can build positive brand signals.

Your Signature Brand Story

A great brand story has a beginning, middle, and turning point:

"I noticed ___, so I decided to try ___. Here's what happened..."

This is how you *talk about* your 10% Project in interviews, intros, bios, or even coffee chats. It makes your work *stick* in people's minds—and it shows who you are without ever having to "brag."

Building Your Brand: 8 Brand Signals That Attract Opportunities

To create a personal brand that resonates, think about the qualities you want to be known for. What do people love to be around? What qualities create magnetism?

Here are some brand elements that make people naturally attractive and respected:

- **Positive Attitude**
  Be the person who brings good energy into the room.

- **Curiosity**
  Show an eagerness to learn and explore new ideas.

- **Proactivity**
  Don't wait to be told—jump in and make things happen.

- **Reliability**
  Follow through on your commitments, no matter how small.

- **Creativity**
  Bring fresh perspectives to the table.

- **Leadership**
  Inspire and motivate others through your actions –
  Help others grow.

- **Authenticity**
  Be genuine and true to your values.

- **Generosity**
  Share your knowledge, time, and encouragement
  freely.

Your 10% Project is a chance to intentionally highlight 2–3 (or more) of these attributes. When people see these traits in you, they *want* to work with you, refer you, and help you succeed.

Turning Projects into Perception Shifts

When you start a 10% Project, you're actively crafting your brand. You're no longer just a name on a roster or a face in the crowd—you're the person who makes things happen. Whether your project is professional, personal, or community-focused, it becomes a reflection of who you are and what you value.

Here's how to turn your project into a brand amplifier:

1. **Define Your Personal Brand**
   What three words do you want people to associate with you?

2. **Pick a Project That Proves Them**
   Your 10% Project should naturally highlight the qualities you want to emphasize. Example: If you want to be seen as "strategic," don't just write blog posts (unless they are about strategy) —analyze a system and improve it

3. **Tell Your Story**
   Share progress, insights, and outcomes. Whether it's on social media, in meetings, or through a simple email update, keep people in the loop.

4. **Invite Collaboration**
   Let others see that you value their input. It shows openness and teamwork.

5. **Stay Consistent**
   One successful 10% Project won't redefine your brand overnight, but a pattern of proactive, interesting projects will. One post is interesting. Five posts is a pattern. Ten is a reputation.

Making It Visible Without Feeling Awkward

Not everyone loves self-promotion. Good news—you don't have to "brag." Try sharing:

- What you're learning.
- What you're testing.
- Who you're collaborating with.
- Where you hit friction and how you work through it.

Use starter phrases like:

- "This was fun to build…"
- "Here's something I learned this week…"
- "Not perfect, but I'm proud of this…"

That's how you show progress *without posturing.*

Attracting the Right People

Great personal branding doesn't just elevate you—it creates connection.

- A shared interest.
- A topic someone's curious about.
- A vibe people want to follow.

Suddenly, your 10% Project isn't just a side effort—it's your *calling card.* As you progress, you bring mentors, collaborators, and champions into your orbit. That's more than networking—it's aligned resonance.

Let Your Project Tell the Story

You don't need a logo or a tagline. You need consistency, curiosity, and a project that reflects what matters to you.

Let your 10% Project be a glimpse into your values. Let it show the energy, care, and creativity you bring to the world.

Because the truth is, you already have a brand.
The question is: **Are you shaping it on purpose?**

CHAPTER 23

Gaining New Experiences

Say Yes to What's Next

The Real Magic of a 10% Project? Unexpected Adventures.

One of the most powerful aspects of a 10% Project is how it pushes you out of your comfort zone and into new experiences. When you start a 10% Project, the real reward often isn't the project itself—it's everything that happens along the way.

Whether it's talking to someone you wouldn't normally approach, experimenting with a new technique, or diving into a completely different field.

Every step outside your routine expands your world. You learn, stretch, connect, grow. You build a richer version of yourself.

Experiences shape who you are—they challenge your perspectives, introduce you to new ideas, and, most importantly, they help keep your mind open, curious and excited about what else might be possible.

Why Say Yes to New Experiences?

We often stick to familiar routines because they're safe and predictable. But when you take the leap to try something unfamiliar, you unlock new ways of thinking and fresh perspectives. Experiences make you richer—not just in knowledge, but in how you see the world. They teach you adaptability, resilience, and creativity. Plus, they're just plain fun! Imagine looking back and realizing that a small project led to meeting fascinating people, discovering a new passion, or even changing your career path.

Growth doesn't live in the comfortable. It lives on the edges—where you try new things, meet new people, and say, "Sure, why not?" When you take the leap to try something unfamiliar... Every time you explore unfamiliar territory, you unlock new parts of yourself. Curiosity grows. Confidence grows. Life grows.

You gain skills, stories, and perspective—and a life that's more exciting.

Saying Yes When It's Easier to Say No

When I was offered the opportunity to relocate to the United States, I was both excited and absolutely terrified.

Yes, it sounded like a dream — a new job, new city, new country, new adventures. But in reality? It meant leaving behind a lifetime of friends, family, relationships, and the comfort of a familiar rhythm. I was stepping into a new country, a new company, a new role, and a whole new career — completely on my own.

I remember packing up everything I owned while playing Kylie Minogue's song "Jump" on repeat. The chorus — "I run to the future and jump" — felt like a direct line to my heart. It became my unofficial anthem as I said farewell to everything I knew and leapt into the unknown.

And I did it. I made the jump. I found new, amazing friends. I built a career that was beyond anything I imagined. And I had a whole lot of fun along the way.

Sometimes the scariest leap you take ends up being the most important one.

You don't always feel ready. You just have to *jump.*

Your Project Is Just the Starting Line

You might think you're building a small idea—but you're really building a bigger version of yourself & your life. 10% Projects have a way of opening doors to unexpected opportunities.

Maybe your 10% Project to learn basic coding leads to collaborating with a tech enthusiast who introduces you to app development. Perhaps your idea to organize a community event leads you to meet a local leader who becomes a mentor. The 10% Project itself is just the start—the experiences it leads to are often the real reward.

You meet fascinating people. You discover new industries. You realize, "Wait—I'm actually *good* at this."

The outcome matters—but the *experience* of doing something new? That's what sticks with you. That's where the magic is.

10% Projects Expand Your World

- **Talk to New People**
  One of the simplest ways to expand your experience is to reach out and start conversations. Your 10% Project can be the perfect icebreaker.

- **Experiment**
  Even if your 10% Project doesn't succeed at first, experimenting builds your problem-solving skills.

- **Stretch Creatively**
  Choose a 10% Project that challenges you creatively, whether it's designing, writing, or inventing something new. Give yourself permission to try crazy ideas.

- **Seek Out Collaboration**
  Working with others not only shares the workload but also exposes you to different ways of thinking. Other people = new lenses, faster learning, and more fun.

The Ripple Effect: How Experiences Expand Your World

The more experiences you gain, the more you'll notice how one thing leads to another. Curiosity sparks action, action brings new insights, and those insights open doors you never knew were available. You start seeing opportunities everywhere because your mindset shifts from routine to exploration.

New ideas spark more new ideas. You'll notice patterns, insights, and opportunities popping up where you used to see routine.

You train your brain to spot possibility - instead of limitation. And that changes *everything*.

You're Not "Built Differently" – It's the way you train yourself.

When I was talking to a freind about the early version of this concept, she said something that stopped me in my tracks:

"You see opportunities everywhere. I think some people are just built like that. Most people don't think that way."

And I get it. From the outside, it might look like I've always been wired to spot possibilities. But I don't believe I was born that way. I trained that way.

It's not some genetic default — it's decades of doing 10% Projects. Every time I took on something new, curious, or just slightly outside my lane, I strengthened the part of my brain that says, "What if...?" instead of "Probably not."

The more 10% Projects you do — your first, your second, your third — the more your brain starts catching sparks in places you used to overlook. And eventually, people will say things like, "Wow, you're so creative" or "You always find a way."

But it's not magic.
It's practice.
And it's available for anyone who's willing to start.

Why It's Worth the Effort

It's easy to play it safe, but safe often means stagnant. Embracing new experiences makes life richer and more fulfilling. Every new experience you gather becomes a building block in your personal and professional life. You become that person who always has a story to share, a lesson learned, or a fresh idea to pitch.

Safe is... well, safe. But new experiences make you interesting. Resilient. Fulfilled. You become the kind of person who people want to know, follow, and work with.

The Experience Is the Win

Don't be afraid to take that first step into the unknown. Talk to the person. Sketch the idea. Press send. Even if it doesn't work out the way you imagined, the growth is already yours. Always "run to the future and jump".

Your 10% Project is more than a to-do. It's an invitation. Your 10% Project is the vehicle that drives you into new territory, where you can grow, learn, and thrive. Keep your mind open, your heart curious, and your willingness to explore intact.

Say yes to it. And see where it leads.

This moment felt riskier than any project.

I'll be honest: one of the scariest moments of this whole journey wasn't taking on new opportunities — it was standing up in front of my team at work and presenting this book.

It wasn't just a concept. It was me. My approach to work, my career, to life, to what I believe really matters. It felt like putting my heart on display.

I was terrified they'd think it was fluffy, or self-indulgent, or too different.

But I did it anyway. And something amazing happened: they leaned in. They saw me. And it opened a whole new level of connection and credibility I never expected.

The "How Hard Can It Be?" Mindset

Imagine this: You hit a challenge and instead of freezing or feeling overwhelmed, you shrug and say, "How hard can it be?" That little phrase? It's a game-changer.

It flips fear into curiosity—and opens the door to growth.

Embracing new skills isn't just a career move—it's a life philosophy. It keeps your mind sharp, your spirit curious, and your world full of possibility.

The real blocker? Fear of failing or looking foolish. But here's the truth: nobody's born knowing everything. Everyone starts at zero.

When you approach life as a forever-learner, everything becomes a chance to level up. Your brain buzzes. Your confidence builds. You surprise yourself.

"How hard can it be?" comes into play whenever you might be tempted to back away from something unfamiliar or intimidating. Instead of letting doubt take over, break the challenge down into smaller, more manageable pieces. The first step is often the hardest, but once you start, you realize it's not as daunting as it seemed.

That's exactly what a 10% Project is all about—taking on something new, breaking it down, and moving forward step by step. You're not committing to reinventing your whole life. You're just saying: *"I'll give this a shot. Just 10%. Just enough to learn something new."* You don't need to overhaul your life—just carve out a little room to grow.

Doing more of what you love, means doing it well, because you do it with passion and commitment. Ultimately that action will attract more of what you love to you.

Why Should You Keep Building Your Skills?

Here's why continuous growth matters:

- **Future-Proofing**
  The world is constantly evolving, and keeping your skills fresh makes you adaptable.

- **Personal Fulfillment**
  Learning something new gives you a sense of accomplishment.

- **Career Advancement**
  Being the person who's always expanding their knowledge makes you extremely valuable.

- **Increased Confidence**
  Each new skill you master boosts your self-belief and resilience.

- **Unlocking Opportunities**
  Sometimes, learning one new thing opens doors you never expected.

New Skills = New Joy

New skills aren't just useful; they're fun. Whether it's learning to play the guitar, figuring out data analysis, or mastering public speaking, every small win feels good. It's like giving yourself a mental high-five.

186 | THE 10% PROJECT

Real-World Skills That Spark Growth

- ⚙ **Communication**
  Speak clearly, confidently, and with purpose - Taking a public speaking class or joining a debate group.

- ⚙ **Technical Proficiency**
  Learning a new software that's relevant to your job - Learn one new program that makes work smoother.

- ⚙ **Creativity**
  Take up design, writing, or art just for the joy of it - Pick up a craft to start a small business, learn a new art form and hold a show, or master a musical instrument and start a band. New skills and experiences lead to new networks.

- ⚙ **Social Skills**
  Improving your ability to network and connect with others – meet new people in areas that interest you.

- ⚙ **Problem-Solving**
  Practicing new approaches to old challenges - Try a new approach to something that's always annoyed you.

Unexpected Upside: Where Skills Take You

Here's the twist: you might start learning for one reason, and find it helping in a totally different way.

- ⚙ **Learning to code** - automating that mind-numbing spreadsheet.
- ⚙ **Practicing storytelling** - making you a more engaging presenter.
- ⚙ **Taking up graphic design** - making killer pitch decks.
- ⚙ **Public speaking** - nailing that promotion interview.

Keep Rolling—Even When It Feels Slow

Once you've taken the first step, keep pushing. The more you practice, the easier it becomes. Eventually, you'll look back and realize how much you've grown without even noticing.

Momentum builds from micro moves. Even 10 minutes counts. Before you know it, you'll look back and think, "Whoa, I *can* do this."

Be a Work-in-Progress, Proudly

You're not meant to be done. Ever. You're meant to keep stretching, playing, tinkering, growing... always.

Let your 10% Project be your playground. Pick something weird. Something cool. Something that reminds you—*you're not done yet.* Because really—how hard can it be, right?

CHAPTER 24

Embracing Risk

Even if you're scared

The Leap of Faith

You've done the hard work. You've invested in yourself. You've built momentum through a 10% Project. And then... it happens. A new opportunity appears. It's exciting. And terrifying.

Maybe it's a new job in a new industry. Maybe it's a big shift in direction. Maybe it's simply saying yes to something that feels *bigger than you.* Your gut tightens. Your brain fills with "what ifs."

That's normal.

Big opportunities *always* come with fear. That doesn't mean they're wrong—it means they're *real.*

Fear ≠ Danger: Learning to Feel It Without Freezing

Let's be clear: Fear is not a failure. It's not a weakness. It's not a sign to stop.

It's your brain trying to protect you. But often, it's overprotecting you.

Fear shows up when something matters. It's not the enemy—it's a compass.

Try this quick flip: Instead of "I'm scared because I might fail," say: "I'm scared because I care—and I'm about to grow."

Imposter Syndrome Is a Liar

Here's something most people don't say out loud: The more you grow, the more likely you are to feel like a fraud. You're not. You're expanding. That's what makes it feel wobbly.

Let's break down a few classic lies we can tell ourselves and replace them with truths:

Imposter thought	Reframe
"I'm not ready yet."	You're not supposed to be ready. You're supposed to be willing.
"I don't belong here."	You're new, not unworthy. Belonging comes with action.
"I'm going to fail."	Maybe. But you'll learn faster—and rise stronger. Taking the first step is what counts.

Real Talk

When Fear Meets a Microphone
How I turned a stutter—and a stereotype—into a platform for leadership

When I moved to the U.S. alone for a new job—new country, new company, new role—I didn't just face fear. I collided with it. I've had a stutter my whole life. And this new role? It required me to get up and teach leadership and marketing to senior leaders at Boeing's corporate university. It was terrifying.

The week I arrived, my first day on the job, someone told me—'kindly' but firmly—that I'd never succeed in the company unless I could fix my stutter. She didn't realize it was a disability, and I couldn't simply 'fix' it. I sat down, alone, and cried.

But I didn't stay there. With the help of a coach named Linda Bailey (I'll never forget her), I shifted from 'I can't do this, I'm going home to Australia.' to 'Damn it—I'll show them I can.

That was over 20 years ago. Since then, I've gone on to lead, teach, and speak for major companies—including Boeing, Qualcomm and Adobe, multiple startup companies, and at events around the world. And now, I've written this book to share my stories and what I've learned. Because fear doesn't get to decide what I do. I do.

Weighing the Risks (and the Reality)

Sometimes the fear isn't just in your head. Maybe you've got kids, financial pressures, aging parents, or other life factors that make risk feel... risky.

Here's where you pause—not to say no, but to make a plan.

Try a reflection grid:

- What's the best-case scenario?
  What's the worst-case realistic outcome?
- What would I gain either way?
  What might I regret if I don't try?

This helps you shift from "catastrophe thinking" to thoughtful courage.

Stretch Without Snapping

Courage doesn't mean jumping off a cliff. It means taking bold, thoughtful steps. You don't have to say yes to everything immediately.

You can:

- Test the waters
- Ask more questions
- Build a skill first

- Try a side project version

Risk doesn't have to be reckless. It just has to be understood, managed, and handled rationally.

Confidence Isn't the Absence of Doubt

Confidence isn't knowing everything from the start. It's believing you have what it takes to figure things out as you go.

No one has all the answers when they step into a new role, and that's okay. Feeling nervous is a natural part of the process—it means you're stepping out of your comfort zone. Embrace that feeling as a sign that you're growing. Confidence doesn't mean you never doubt yourself; it means you push forward despite the doubt.

In reality, no one expects you to be perfect on day one. Employers and colleagues know that every new position comes with a learning curve. The important thing is to stay open, be willing to learn, and trust your own capacity to adapt. Your past successes, including your 10% Projects, have already proven your resilience and commitment. Let that track record fuel your confidence.

No One Expects Perfection on Day One. They Expect Willingness

Confidence is the willingness to learn. To try. To ask for help. Confidence isn't "I've got this."... It's "I'll find a way".

Think back to before starting your 10% Project:

- You didn't know everything when you started.
- You made it up as you went.
- You kept going.

That's what confidence *looks* like.

Playing It Safe Can Be a Risk, Too

It's easy to stay where it's comfortable. But comfort can become a cage. What looks "safe" now might feel stagnant later.

Ask yourself:
"Five years from now, what might I wish I had said yes to?"

Sometimes the biggest risk is not growing, and staying exactly where you are.

From 10% Project to Bold Leap

You've been practicing courage already. Every idea you explored, every challenge you took on, every tiny risk you tested in your 10% Projects—it was all training.

So when the big opportunity comes? You're ready. Even if you don't feel like it.

Remind yourself:

- You've solved hard problems before.
- You've shown up for growth before.
- You don't need to be fearless. You just need to *start.*

A Risk I Want to Take Anyway

Try this courage mini-plan:

1. Something I want but feel scared to pursue:
   Write it down...

2. **What I'm afraid will happen:**
   Name the fear—out loud. It loses power when you name it.

3. **Why it's still worth it:**
   Find the deeper "why." What will you gain even if it's messy?

You don't have to jump today. But maybe take one step.

Fighting Self-Doubt

People who see your work on a 10% Project, see how you stretched yourself and leant into learning, will be more likely to think you can handle a new opportunity as well. Don't let self-doubt limit you. By taking on a 10% Project, you've already shown yourself and those around you what kind of person you are: resilient, resourceful, and committed. Now is the time to grab that opportunity with both hands, run toward the future, and take the leap. Have faith in yourself.

Leveraging Your Skills and Brand

Believe in yourself and live up to the brand you've carefully created. If others have enough confidence in you to place an incredible opportunity in your path, you need to have the confidence to take it. Reflect on what your 10% Projects have shown about your abilities: your willingness to take risks, learn new skills, and persist through challenges. Use these experiences as your foundation to tackle new opportunities.

Treating Every Opportunity as a Learning Experience

Everything is a learning process—treat your new opportunity in the same way you embraced your 10% Projects. Break things down, identify the skills or experiences you need, and go get them. Be open to asking for help, seeking expertise, and building the network necessary for success.

Embracing a Growth Mindset

Don't let imposter syndrome become a self-inflicted barrier. Remember, everyone starts somewhere, and it's okay to not know everything from the outset. Your willingness to learn and adapt is far more valuable than innate talent. You can do it!

Brave Isn't Perfect—It's Willing

Taking risks is never easy, but it is an essential part of personal and professional growth. Embrace the discomfort, acknowledge the fear, and push forward. You've already proven your potential through your commitment to your 10% Projects—now it's time to use that momentum to achieve even greater things. Taking on a new challenge is not about being fearless; it's about moving forward despite fear. Be proud of your courage to embrace risk and thrive.

Taking risks doesn't mean you stop being scared.

- It means you do it *while* being scared.
- It means you bet on yourself.
- It means you say: "I might not know how yet... but I will."

The Power of 'Yet'.

That one little word holds a surprising amount of courage: *yet*. It's only three letters long, but it builds a bridge between where you are and where you want to be. "I can't do that" becomes "I can't do that *yet*." "I'm not good at this" becomes "I'm not good at this *yet*." That one small shift changes a closed door into a path forward.

Yet is permission to be a work in progress. It's proof that growth is still possible. That learning is still happening. That courage doesn't require mastery—it just requires movement.

When you're facing risk or uncertainty 'yet' becomes a quiet but powerful companion. It reminds you that you don't have to have it all figured out right now. You just have to believe that you can take the next step—and that your future self is capable of even more.

So when self-doubt whispers, "You're not ready," answer back with: "Maybe not *yet*... but I'm getting there."

That's what brave looks like. And that's how you keep going.

You don't need to feel 100% ready. You just need to be 10% braver than your doubt.

Let's go!

CHAPTER 25

Staying Optimistic

Why Every Project Is a Win (Even if It Flops)

When Projects Don't Go as Planned

Not every 10% Project is going to set the world on fire. Sometimes, despite all your time, passion, sticky notes, and borderline delusional optimism... it flops. Or fizzles. Or vanishes in a sad little puff of "meh." And you know what? That's totally okay.

The real power of a 10% Project isn't in whether it *worked*. It's in the fact that *you worked it.*

You showed up. You tried. You learned. You grew. That's never, ever wasted.

You're Growing Even When It Feels Like You're Failing

Here's what happens every time you take on a 10% Project—whether it ends with fireworks or just some polite clapping:

- You stretched your brain.
- You stress-tested your creativity.
- You flexed your courage muscles.
- You got clearer on what actually matters to you

Those subtle shifts? That's the gold. Even if the whole thing feels like a beautiful mess... *you* worked. And that matters.

The Real Wins: Invisible but Invaluable

A 10% Project changes you. You become more confident, engaged, happier, more enthusiastic, and more hopeful. You learn to tackle challenges head-on and develop a stronger sense of purpose.

Sometimes, these changes aren't apparent right away. You might be so caught up in the Project itself that you miss how you've grown. But when you look back, you'll be surprised at how much you've accomplished and how your actions set the stage for where you are now.

Here's what every 10% Project gives you—even the weird, wonky, wildly unfinished ones:

- **Increased Confidence**
  Taking on a new challenge shows you can step out of your comfort zone. You learn to take on challenges without knowing all the answers upfront. You step up when no one makes you.

- **Enhanced Problem-Solving Skills**
  You learn to think creatively and adapt, to develop creative solutions when facing obstacles. You solve problems you didn't even realize were issues yet.

- **Broader Network**
  You connect with people who support your growth. You meet new people who share your interests or can support your goals. You meet people through the spark of your idea.

- **Greater Resilience**
  You learn to handle setbacks without losing motivation. You learn to bounce back faster when things don't go as planned. You keep going when it gets awkward.

- **Improved Communication**
  You get better at sharing your ideas and collaborating with others.

- **Personal Growth**
  You become more self-aware and better at self-motivation.

These might not go on your resume—but they do significantly upgrade your life. Every single time.

Not Everything is Yours to Control (And Actually That's a Gift)

It's tempting to judge a project by the outcome. But you can't control the timing. You can't control who "gets it." You can't control whether your workplace adopts your idea or your family cheers you on.

What you *can* control?

- Showing up.
- Trying something.
- Learning something.
- Staying open to what's next.

That's more than enough.

You don't need applause—or permission—to feel proud of your effort.

Why Projects "Fail" (Spoiler: It's Probably Not You)

There are many reasons why a 10% Project might not reach the outcome you envisioned.

Here's your friendly reality check on why things go sideways sometimes:

- **Timing was off**
  You were probably ahead of your time.
  That's not failure, that's visionary.

- **People didn't jump on board**
  That's their limitation—not a reflection of your brilliance.

- **Resources were thin**
  Ideas need fuel. Under-resourcing isn't the same as a crash and burn.

- **Evolving Goals**
  You're growing.
  So your goals should evolve.

The Humor of It All: Laugh at the Chaos

Some 10% Projects don't just fail—they crash-land in flames and leave behind stories you'll tell for *years.*

- Like the time your "genius new process" took down the entire printer network for two days.
- Or when your "fun snack-themed icebreaker" ended in 5 allergic reactions.
- Or the pitch deck that boldly featured the *wrong client's name* on every single slide.

Those moments? They're not failures. They're *material.* For TED talks, team huddles, or at the very least, happy hour.

Laughing at these moments, while learning from them, doesn't mean you're not taking them seriously; it means you're resilient enough to find joy in the process.

Optimism isn't just joy—it's resilience with a grin.

Celebrate the Process Like You Would the Win

It's easy to celebrate when your project goes viral or gets funded. But the real power move? Clapping for yourself just for starting. Just for staying in it. Just for trying.

Did you keep going even when no one clapped? Stay curious when things got weird? Build something out of scraps and stubbornness?

That's heroic. That's worth celebrating.

Don't wait for success to give yourself permission to feel proud. Don't wait for "success" to hand yourself a gold star. You've earned it just by daring to begin.

Keep a 10% Graveyard (Yes, Really)

Never toss out an idea forever. Instead, start a folder—a "10% Graveyard" if you like the drama, or "Idea Vault" if you're feeling hopeful.

Fill it with:

- Project decks that didn't quite land (yet).
- Half-finished outlines and brainstorms.
- Things you *almost* finished.
- Ideas you abandoned halfway through (for now).

Why bother?

- Because ideas resurface.
- People might show up later who want to co-create.
- And your future self might see magic in something old.

Dead ideas? Never... They're just napping.

The Process Matters Just as Much as the Result

Never forget... The true value of a 10% Project lies in the process—how you push yourself to innovate, think differently, act creatively, and stay persistent. Sometimes it's not about the end result; it's about the skills, the mindset, and the confidence you build along the way. That growth is invaluable.

A New Perspective: From "Success" to "Seeds"

Try this reframe:
"Even if this doesn't grow, it plants something."

A connection. A new skill. A story you'll tell later. Sometimes the impact is slow release. Sometimes it takes a season. But when it blooms? You'll be glad you planted it.

Stay Light, Stay Brave, Stay You

The secret to staying optimistic isn't pretending everything's fine—it's choosing to *find meaning* even when it's not.

It's saying:

- "Well... that went sideways." and still laughing.
- "Oof, that hurt." and still growing.
- "Let's try again." because you know you're worth the effort.

Celebrate your courage. Keep going. And whatever happens—keep laughing. Your future self is already raising a glass to this version of you.

"The only limit
to our realization of tomorrow
will be our doubts of today."

Franklin D. Roosevelt

SECTION 6
Red Flags

CHAPTER 26

Opportunity Killers

What's Holding You Back?

Facing the Tough Truth

You've built your 10% Project Plan, taken the leap, and maybe even started strong... but still, the opportunities aren't showing up. That's real—and frustrating.

Before you assume it's the system, your boss, or just bad luck, it's worth asking: *Am I unintentionally blocking my own momentum?*

In this chapter, we'll dig into the most common "opportunity killers"— self-sabotaging habits that can quietly undermine all your efforts.

The good news? Once you spot them, you can fix them. And when you do, your 10% Project becomes not just a passion play—but a launch pad.

The Four Biggest Opportunity Killers

1. Not Documenting Your Efforts

One of the most significant opportunity killers is failing to document your progress and achievements. No matter how much effort you put into your 10% Project, if there's no record of your progress, it's as if it never happened.

If it's not documented, it didn't happen.

That might sound harsh, but in most organizations, visibility equals value. If no one can *see* your 10% Project in action, they won't know what you've built—or why it matters.

Why This Kills Opportunity

People are busy. Your manager might support your growth in theory, but unless you're tracking and sharing what you're doing, your progress becomes invisible.

What to Document (The 10% Way):

- Your original goal or hypothesis.
- Tangible actions taken.
- Feedback received and how you applied it.
- Impact, outcomes, or lessons learned.

Keep a simple a one-page document you update biweekly. It becomes your proof of momentum and your script for updates.

2. Not Investing Your Time

A 10% Project that's never worked on? That's just a daydream. The difference between dabbling and momentum is *dedicated time.* If you only touch your project when the stars align, it's not going to grow.

The Fix:

- Put it on your calendar—weekly, just like a meeting.
- Break the work into 15, 30 or 60 minute sprints.
- Set visible micro-goals so you stay motivated.

- Share your progress with your mentor or manager to stay accountable.

This isn't just extra credit. It's a strategic career move. *Treat it like one.*

3. Seeing Your Project as Just a Benefit to the Company

It's easy to fall into the trap of designing your project purely as a value add for your employer rather than as a developmental opportunity for yourself.

When your 10% Project is only about helping the company, you miss the best part: **your growth**.

Yes, it should be valuable to others—but the magic happens when it also challenges, stretches, and develops *you.*

Reframe it like this:

This project helps our organization do X, and it helps me build Y.

Example:

"I'm building a new onboarding guide (org win) while developing my instructional design and cross-team influence skills (personal win)."

This is a 10% Project. It's meant to light *you* up.

4. Not Taking Feedback Seriously

Feedback isn't failure—it's fuel. But only if you use it.

People notice when you listen, adjust, and improve. They also notice when you brush it off. One builds trust—the other kills momentum.

Do this instead:

- Invite feedback early and often.
- Say *"thank you,"* not *"yeah, but..."*
- Follow up later: *"Hey, I took your advice and changed X—it really helped. Thank you."*

Use feedback to *evolve* your 10% Project in public. It shows humility, agility, and leadership in action.

Addressing Other Opportunity Killers

While the four above are the major culprits, there are a few other behaviors that can also hinder your progress:

- **Being Inconsistent:** Sporadic effort undermines your credibility.
  Inconsistent effort = *"They're not serious".*

- **Lack of Follow-Up:** Not updating your manager or mentor makes it seem like your project has stalled.
  No follow-up = *"Guess it fizzled out".*

- **Focusing Solely on Short-Term Gains:** Great projects often take time. If you're constantly looking for immediate results, you might abandon valuable initiatives prematurely.
  Only chasing quick wins = *"Shiny, not strategic".*

Turnaround a Play (in action):

Imagine you've started a 10% project aimed at improving team collaboration. You worked on it for a few weeks, but feedback from your manager suggests that the team doesn't really understand the value of what you're doing.

Rather than feeling frustrated, you take a step back and:

1. **Document real outcomes:** Less back-and-forth, faster decisions.

2. **Gather feedback:** What's working, what's fuzzy.

3. **Reframe + re-message:** Show how it supports the bigger goals. Make adjustments based on feedback and clearly communicate the positive changes.

4. **Loop back:** Share results with leadership and mentor.

By actively listening, documenting progress, and showing your willingness to adapt, you turn a potential failure into an opportunity to strengthen your project—and your reputation.

Result? You turn resistance into recognition—and show real leadership under pressure.

Avoiding Self-Sabotage

The truth is, sometimes we can be our own worst enemies when it comes to creating opportunities. The good news? Once you identify what's holding you back, you have the power to fix it. Be honest with yourself, make the necessary adjustments, and turn those opportunity killers into opportunity makers.

Every 10% Project has two sides: what you *build*—and what might be quietly breaking it. When you name and fix the habits that kill momentum, you open the door for real visibility, trust, and opportunity.

This isn't about being perfect. It's about staying aware, staying committed, and staying in motion. You've got this. Flip those killers into catalysts—and keep going.

CHAPTER 27

Current Perceptions of You

And How to Change Them

Why Perception Matters

You might be doing excellent work—but if no one *sees* it, or if they misunderstand your intent, it can quietly stall your momentum.

In workplace dynamics, **perception is currency**. Whether accurate or not, how you're seen shapes how you're treated—and how opportunities flow.

Here's the good news: perception is **malleable**. You can reshape how others see you by being intentional, reflective, and a little strategic. Let's get into how.

STEP ONE: UNDERSTAND HOW YOU'RE PERCEIVED

Finding out how others see you isn't always straightforward. People tend to avoid giving negative feedback, especially if they're worried about hurting your feelings or damaging your relationship. But without that honest input, you'll never know what needs to change.

Self-awareness isn't always enough. You need **mirrors—** honest, diverse, and safe reflections of how others see you.

How to Get Honest Feedback

Direct Conversations

- Approach trusted colleagues or mentors and ask for candid feedback.

- Be specific: "I'm working on developing my professional image—how do you think I'm perceived in the team?"

- Ask, "What's one thing I could do differently to be more effective?"

Anonymous Surveys

- Use tools like Google Forms or SurveyMonkey to gather feedback without putting anyone on the spot.

360-Degree Reviews

- These formal tools gather insights from managers, peers, and direct reports, offering a well-rounded view of your strengths and areas for improvement.

- This can reveal patterns or behaviors you might not have noticed.

Personality and Behavior Assessments

- Tools like the Birkman Method can help you understand how your behavior changes under stress and how it may affect your workplace interactions.

The Power of Personality Assessments

Personality tools like Birkman not only measure your typical behavior but also how you react under stress. Understanding these shifts can help you recognize when your stress reactions might be sabotaging your efforts.

Identifying these patterns can help you develop coping strategies to maintain your professional demeanor, even when pressure mounts.

For example:

- **Normal Behavior**
  Collaborative and communicative.

- **Stress Behavior**
  Withdrawn and defensive.

Personality Tools

There are plenty of assessment tools out there... here are a couple that I've worked with that I have found really helpful.

- **Birkman Method** – great for spotting stress behaviors and communication styles.

- **MBTI (Myers-Briggs)** – helps surface natural work preferences (e.g., ENFJ, ISTP, etc.).

- **DISC or StrengthsFinder** – simple, powerful language for describing how you work.

Use tools *plus* conversations. One gives data. The other gives context.

STEP TWO: CREATE A PLAN TO ADDRESS PERCEPTION ISSUES

Once you've identified the gaps between how you're seen and how you want to be seen, it's time to take action.

Now you know how you're perceived vs. how you *want* to be, it's time to create your image so you become seen the way you really want to be seen – the way you really are.

Perception Shift Plan

Checklist for Changing Perceptions:

- **Acknowledge the Feedback**

- Thank people for being honest, even if it's hard to hear.
- Don't deflect—say thank you.

Analyze the Patterns

- Are multiple people mentioning the same issue? Focus on those areas first.
- If 3 people say you seem reserved... believe them.

Set Concrete Goals

- Identify specific behaviors to change. For example, if you're seen as unapproachable, practice open body language and more inclusive communication.
- Instead of "be more outgoing," say "be perceived as approachable and collaborative."

Develop a Communication Plan

- Regularly update your manager or team on your progress.
- Use phrases like,
  "I've been working on being more collaborative. Have you noticed any improvements?"

Seek Coaching

- Professional coaches can provide strategies for building a positive professional image.
- You don't have to do it alone.

Track Your Progress

- Keep a record of positive feedback or changes you've implemented. This can serve as evidence when discussing your development with your manager.

- Save notes, emails, or examples of feedback shifts.

STEP THREE: MAKE YOUR WORK VISIBLE

In some cases, it's not a perception problem—it's a **visibility gap**. People can't value what they don't see.

Sometimes, it's not that you're perceived negatively—it's that you're not perceived at all. Being unnoticed can feel just as frustrating as being misjudged.

Strategies to Increase Your Visibility

- Regular Reporting
  - Create consistent, concise updates that show your progress and accomplishments.
  - Monthly updates that summarize progress and outcomes.

- Metrics That Matter
  - Identify key performance indicators (KPIs) that demonstrate your value. For example, how much time you save through improved processes.
  - Focus on impact—not just activity.

- Show the Impact - the "What If"
  - Create reports that highlight what would happen if your work weren't being done.
  - Frame your role as essential to team success.
  - What would fall apart without your work? Make that visible.

- Share Wins Casually
  - Don't just do good work—make sure others know about it.

- Share successes during team meetings or via email updates.

- "Hey, the process we tried last sprint worked really well— it cut processing time by 25%."

Visibility isn't bragging. It's *advocacy*. And it starts with you.

STEP FOUR: MAKE SELF IMPROVEMENT YOUR FIRST 10% PROJECT

Perception shifting is one of the most powerful 10% Projects you can do.

It's personal, actionable, and highly visible when done right.

Make it structured.

If you discover that your current perception at work isn't what you'd like, make changing it your first 10% Project.

Approach it with the same structure and determination as any other personal development initiative.

- **Set Clear Goals**

- **Define Your Ideal Reputation**
  - What 3 words do you want people to associate with you?
  - Define how you want to be seen: competent, reliable, collaborative?

- **Build Micro-Actions**
  - If one of them is "strategic," how do you show that weekly?

- **Loop in a Mentor**
  - Use Your Personal Growth Map to get feedback on how your shift is landing.

- **Track Behavior Shifts**
  - Weekly: what you tried, what landed, and what you'll tweak.

Owning Your Professional Story

Perception is fluid. You don't need to overhaul your personality—you just need to align how you show up with who you actually are.

Own your reputation. Shape it on purpose. And if it's off-track? Use feedback, frameworks, and 10% Projects to bring it back in line with the leader you're becoming.

"The quality of your life
is the quality
of your relationships."

Tony Robbins

SECTION 7
Connections

CHAPTER 28

Networking

Building Genuine Connections

Why Networking Matters in Your 10% Project

A 10% Project doesn't live in a vacuum. The most powerful growth doesn't just come from what you build — it comes from **who sees it, who supports it,** and **who joins you along the way**. That's why networking isn't optional; it's foundational. Not the transactional kind of networking — but real connection-building that helps your ideas travel, evolve, and gain traction. If your project is the spark, your network is the oxygen. One fuels the other. And when you learn how to build and nurture relationships alongside your 10% Project, the possibilities multiply faster than you'd ever imagine.

How a 10% Project Makes Networking Feel Natural

Here's a secret benefit of a 10% Project: it gives you the perfect reason to talk to people—without any awkwardness. When you're working on something bold, fresh, or personal, you *need* insights. You have an authentic reason to reach out, and that makes conversations easier and more meaningful. People *love* being asked for their perspective. It's flattering, respectful, and relationship-building.

Your 10% Project becomes a *bridge* for ongoing connection. You're not just asking once—you're looping back to share progress, swap ideas, or say thanks. This keeps you present in their minds and builds trust. It's not a one-off "ask." It's an evolving story that includes them. That's how real, lasting connections grow.

This ongoing interaction keeps you top of mind with your network. When an opportunity arises, they're more likely to think of you because the conversation has remained active and positive. It's not just a one-time touchpoint; it's an evolving connection that shows you appreciate their contributions.

The Power of Networking (According to Data)

Let's talk numbers. LinkedIn reports that **85% of jobs** are filled through networking, not cold applications. And employees who network internally? They get promoted faster. Why? Because networking keeps you visible. It puts your name in the right rooms before you even realize there's a room to be in.

It's not just about finding jobs; it's about staying visible, building influence, and being top of mind when opportunities arise.

Beyond promotions and job offers, networking makes you a more dynamic human. Talking with people outside your bubble builds empathy, creativity, and emotional range. Professional growth is great—but personal growth? That's a lifelong return on the investment of your time, energy, and commitment.

Internal vs. External Networking

- **Internal Networking**

  Relationships inside your current company—think cross-department chats, coffee with a senior leader, or joining a project outside your usual lane (or leading that 10% Project you've been planning). It increases visibility and uncovers new opportunities—right where you are. Particularly if you work for a large organization, navigating the organization and cultivating your internal network is critical to creating future opportunities for yourself.

- **External Networking**

  Building relationships outside of your organization, connections beyond your company's walls. This might include attending industry events, joining professional associations, or maintaining connections with past colleagues. External networking helps you stay updated on industry trends and opens career opportunities beyond your current workplace.

It keeps your perspective fresh—and your options open.

How to Start Networking

- **Start Small**
  Begin with familiar faces. Reconnect with someone you already know or share a passion with. A coffee chat is perfect.

- **Be Curious**
  Ask questions about their experiences, challenges, or goals. People love talking about the things they are passionate about. Curiosity builds connection faster than small talk.

- **Follow Up**
  Send a quick "thanks, loved catching up!" afterward. Thoughtfulness is remembered.

- **Offer Value**
  Reciprocity is key. Support goes both ways. Share an article, cheer them on, or send a kind word— especially when you *don't* need anything.

How to Stay Top of Mind

Want to be remembered (in a good way)? Keep your network warm with small, consistent actions.

By actively maintaining and expanding your professional network, you increase the likelihood of being considered for opportunities that are not publicly advertised, thereby enhancing your career progression prospects.

To effectively stay top of mind, consider the following strategies:

- **Go to Industry Events**
  These gatherings provide opportunities to meet professionals in your field and learn about unadvertised positions. Meet new people, learn new things, and get the inside scoop on jobs that never hit the job boards.

- **Use LinkedIn Like a Pro**
  Regularly update your LinkedIn profile, engage with content relevant to your industry, and connect with peers and industry leaders. Keep it fresh. Share updates. Engage with others. Visibility = opportunity.

- **Join Professional Associations**
  Membership in industry-specific organizations can offer networking events and professional development resources. They generally offer access to events, member directories, job boards, and instant street credibility.

- **Request Informational Chats**
  Reach out to professionals in roles or companies you're interested in and ask to learn more about their experiences and seek advice. "I'd love to learn from your experience" is one of the most powerful (and flattering) things you can say.

- **Volunteer or Freelance:**
  Engaging in volunteer work or freelance projects can expand your network and showcase your skills to potential employers. It builds your portfolio, your network, and your reputation—all at once.

How 10% Projects Help Build Relationships

This is where your 10% Project becomes a relationship super-tool. It gives people a front-row seat to your passion, your skills, growth, and your initiative. When you loop others in—by asking for input, sharing updates, or just saying thanks—you keep the connection alive in a meaningful way.

Here's what a 10% Project does for your network:

- **Gives You a Reason to Reach Out**
  You have a reason to reach out, and it feels natural, not forced.

- **Showcases Your Strengths**
  People see you in action. You naturally demonstrate your skills and passion as you discuss your project.

- **Creates Built-In Follow-Ups**
  Following up on the project gives you a built-in reason to reconnect. Updates = reconnecting moments.

- **Builds Gratitude Loops**
  Thanking someone for their help reinforces a positive connection. Thank-you notes leave a lasting impression.

- **Sparks Ongoing Involvement**
  You can reengage them when starting a new project, showing continuity and growth. Keeping the door open for future collaboration.

- **Keeps You Top of Mind**
  The ongoing conversation keeps you memorable within your network, so when opportunities arise, people think of you. You stay active in their world, without being pushy.

Water the Garden

Relationships aren't chores. They're gardens. You don't have to hover over them daily—but a little sunlight and water now and then helps them thrive? That's how things grow. Keep your connections alive with curiosity and care. The support you'll need later is already growing today.

The relationships you build today will become the support system you can rely on in the future. Stay curious, stay grateful, and stay connected.

CHAPTER 29

The Multiplier Effect of a Strong Network

Intentionally Building Your Network

One of the most powerful by products of a 10% Project is how naturally it expands your network. But let's be clear: it's not just a lucky side effect. It's a deliberate outcome that can transform your career and personal growth. Intentional networking means going beyond contact lists. You're building a web of authentic relationships that grows stronger—and more valuable—over time. It helps you help you grow personally and professionally.

Networking might just be the most career-shaping thing you can do. Opportunities don't always go to the most qualified—they go to the most connected. The more people you know (and who know what you care about), the more likely you'll come to mind when something big opens up. Every person you connect with opens doors to dozens more. It's like building a web where every connection can potentially introduce you to a whole new world of possibilities. That's the true multiplier effect.

The Power of Connections: Degrees of Separation

You've probably heard of the "Six Degrees of Separation" theory—that any two people on Earth are just six connections apart. But the groundswell of social media? It's shrunk that number even further. For example, a study of Facebook's social graph found that the average distance between users is just 4.74 degrees. LinkedIn? Even tighter.

On platforms like LinkedIn, these connections are categorized as follows:

- **1st-degree connections:** People you are connected to. People you know directly.

- **2nd-degree connections:** Individuals connected to your 1st-degree connections. Friends-of-friends.

- **3rd-degree connections:** People connected to your 2nd-degree connections. Friends-of-their-friends.

Every new person you meet plugs you into their world. That one introduction? It might link you to hundreds more. The ripple effect is real—and that's how surprising, life-changing opportunities often find you.

Each new connection you make doesn't just expand your immediate network—it links you to the networks of everyone they know. This multiplier effect means that even a single new contact can significantly increase your reach, opening up unexpected opportunities.

Get the 'Jump' on Networking

Watch your network expand with every connection.

And so on and so on...

How a Conversation Became a TEDx Dream

While writing this book, I had a call with Rob, a wonderful leadership coach from The Ohio State MBA program where I speak each year. Rob's been a great supporter over the years — a true First Degree Connection.

I told him about the book I was finishing — the one inspired by Liz, the amazing MBA student who'd heard me speak the year before. I walked him through the 10% Project concept, how it works, and how I hoped it could help more people unlock opportunities in their careers.

The more I shared, the more curious Rob got.
Finally, he said: ***"Sue... you should do a TED Talk on this."***

I was stunned. A TED Talk? That idea had never crossed my mind. But the moment he said it, something clicked. It would be a perfect way to share the 10% Project with more people — and help them take bold, intentional steps toward the lives they want.

Then came the ripple. The networking connections...

Rob introduced me to Bonnie — a Second Degree Connection — who had recently given a TEDx Talk of her own. We had an amazing phone call, and at the end, she offered to connect me to her coach: Geoffrey.

A few days later, I was on the phone with Geoffrey — a Third Degree Connection — and we began planning how I might bring the 10% Project to a TEDx stage in the months ahead.

That story is still unfolding.
But this is how a 10% Project grows:
Not all at once.
Not with a giant leap.
But one small, powerful conversation at a time.

Why Adding Just One Person Can Shift Everything

Research from LinkedIn suggests that second- and third-degree connections are often more valuable than immediate contacts when it comes to career advancement. People are more likely to be referred for jobs by these broader connections. In fact, studies from MIT, Harvard, Stanford, and LinkedIn show that "moderately weak" ties can be more effective in job searches than strong, close-knit relationships.

Why? Because your close connections often know the same people and hear about the same opportunities you do - close friends usually swim in the same circles as you.

In contrast, weaker ties introduce you to entirely new networks, ideas, and perspectives. They bring fresh information, unexpected introductions, and brand-new doors to knock on. Even one new connection can reshape your whole playing field. This demonstrates why intentionally growing your network—even by one person—can have a profound impact on your career and life.

How to Intentionally Build Your Network

- **Be Proactive**
  Don't wait for opportunities to network. Reach out to people you admire and regularly check in with your contacts. Don't wait—initiate. Message that speaker you loved. Say hi after a webinar. Show up where ideas are flying.

- **Keep Track of the People You Meet**
  Consider keeping a file or simple note on each person you meet— Jot down key details: what they love, what you clicked over, what they're working on, key interests, shared topics, or goals they mentioned. It doesn't have to be formal, just enough to jog your memory when you reconnect. Your future-you will thank you.

- ☙ **Listen Like It's Your Job**
  Focus on understanding their perspective. Listening builds trust and uncovers areas of mutual interest. The better you listen, the more insight you gain— and the more trust you build.

- ☙ **Always Follow Up**
  After meeting someone, send a brief message thanking them for their time or sharing a follow-up thought "*Thanks for your insight!*" or "*Here's that link I mentioned.*" It reinforces your connection.

- ☙ **Lead with Generosity**
  Be the person who gives value first. It sets the tone and builds authentic goodwill. Offer help, resources, or connections before asking for anything in return. This builds goodwill and trust.

Your Network Grows with Your 10% Project

The 10% Project is a fantastic way to build your network organically. Instead of forcing connections, you're naturally building them through shared interests and collaborative efforts. This isn't about networking for networking's sake. It's about inviting people into something real you're building. With every share, thank-you, and follow-up, you're strengthening your professional circle—while making the whole journey more human.

Take pride in the relationships you cultivate and make it a habit to nurture them over time. Building genuine connections through your 10% Project will not only support your personal growth but also strengthen your professional community.

Stay connected and appreciate every relationship you've built along the way—they're part of your growth, and they're cheering you forward.

And that's what a great 10% Project does. It makes your growth contagious,

CHAPTER 30

Mentoring

Accelerate Your Growth with Guided Support

Networking vs. Mentoring: Understanding the Distinction

While both networking and mentoring involve building professional relationships, they serve different purposes and require varying levels of commitment. Both mentoring and networking are powerful. But they're not the same.

⊂ **Networking**

Networking is like attending a professional mixer where you exchange business cards and LinkedIn invitations. It's about creating a web of contacts that can provide information, opportunities, and support. These relationships are often broad and may not delve deeply into personal development.

Think of it like planting seeds everywhere. You're exchanging business cards, grabbing coffee, maybe collaborating on a project. It's broad, valuable, and flexible—but sometimes surface-level.

⊂ **Mentoring**

Mentoring on the other hand, is akin to having a personal coach. It involves a deeper, more structured relationship where an experienced individual (usually the mentor) provides guidance, support, and insight to a less experienced person (usually the mentee). This relationship focuses on deeper, long-term personal and professional growth.

Think of mentoring like hiring a personal trainer for your career. A mentor isn't just a connection—they're an active guide. They see your potential, challenge your blind spots, and help you close the gap between where you are and where you're going.

In 10% Project terms

- Networking helps you identify doors.
- Mentoring helps you walk through them— with confidence, support, and clarity.

Why Mentoring Works (Especially Inside a 10% Project)

Mentoring isn't just feel-good career fluff. When it's connected to a clear growth initiative—like a 10% Project—it becomes a *career accelerator*. Here's what mentors bring to the table:

- **Personalized Guidance**
  - Mentors provide tailored advice based on their experiences, helping mentees navigate challenges and make informed decisions.
  - They've been where you're going. Their insights help you dodge 10% Project and career potholes, and move forward faster.

- **Skill Development**
  - Through regular interactions, mentors can help mentees identify and develop essential skills, enhancing their professional competence.
  - They help you sharpen what matters—especially for 10% Projects that really stretch you.

- Confidence Boost
  - Having a mentor's support can boost a mentee's self-assurance, encouraging you to take on new challenges and responsibilities

  - Even when you doubt yourself and perhaps even your 10% Project, they don't. That belief is fuel.

- Expanded Perspectives
  - Mentors can offer new viewpoints and insights, broadening a mentee's understanding of their field or industry.

  - They see things you can't. Biases. Blind spots. Bigger pictures.

- Career Momentum
  - Mentored individuals often experience accelerated career progression.

  - Wharton School of the University of Pennsylvania conducted a study showing that mentees are promoted five times more often than those without mentors, and mentors themselves are six times more likely to be promoted.

The Role of the 10% Project in Mentoring

A 10% Project can be a practical way to address skills gaps identified during mentoring conversations. When a mentor suggests gaining experience in a specific area, finding a 10% Project that focuses on that skill is a tangible step forward. Plus, it gives you something concrete to discuss in follow-up meetings: how you applied their advice and the progress you made.

Make Mentoring Fun

Mentoring is about growth, connection, and shared learning. While it can feel awkward at times, having a framework and focusing on practical steps helps make it more purposeful and rewarding. Don't be afraid to acknowledge challenges and celebrate progress. By making your mentor feel valued and actively applying their advice, you build a relationship that benefits both of you. Embrace mentoring as a dynamic partnership where both sides can learn and grow.

A successful mentoring relationship is a dynamic partnership. While mentors provide guidance, mentees should also actively seek ways to make the relationship valuable to both parties. Be proactive in seeking advice, but also show appreciation and respect for your mentor's time and effort. As you grow, remember to share your successes—it keeps your mentor motivated and invested in your journey.

Why This Is a 10% Project Game-Changer

Most people go to mentors when they feel stuck.

10% Project thinkers?   We go to mentors *when we're building*.

That shift changes everything.

You're not just asking for help—you're inviting someone into a living, evolving process. You're creating the *kind* of growth that's visible, energizing, and contagious.

Mentors love that.   Because they don't just want to answer questions—they want to **see impact**.

A mentor helps you get to where you're going.
A 10% Project gives them something real to walk alongside.

"An investment in knowledge always pays the best interest."

Benjamin Franklin

SECTION 8
Key Take-Aways

CHAPTER 31

The 10% Project Cheat Sheet:

Big Ideas Worth Bookmarking

Too busy to read the whole book? We've all been there.

This is your shortcut to the best ideas, boldest truths, and micro-actions that can move your career, your confidence, and your creative energy forward—starting now.

Each insight is distilled from the book. Use this as your quick-start guide, post-read reminder, or go-to page when you need a nudge.

Starting Strong: What 10% Projects Are All About

- A small, passion-fueled project can reshape your career.
- Even 10% of your time, if used wisely, creates real momentum.
- Pick something meaningful to you—not just what others expect.
- Align it to where you want to grow—not just where you are now.

Choosing the Right Project

- Choose projects that light you up and stretch your skills.
- Think overlap: personal passion + professional growth = sweet spot.
- If it's exciting and a little scary, you're in the right zone.

Setting Goals That Don't Fizzle Out

- Break big ideas into small, doable steps.
- Mix short-term wins with long-term growth.
- Expect the plan to evolve—and let it.

Making Time for Your 10%

- Block the time like a real meeting.
- Use sprints, or whatever keeps momentum alive.
- Done is more valuable than perfect. Every small step counts.

Getting Buy-In from Your Boss

- Frame it as a win-win: your growth = company value.
- Speak their language: outcomes, skills, alignment.
- Be flexible. Show that you're serious and coachable.

Building a Network Around Your Project

- Invite collaborators, not just cheerleaders.
- Share progress—it creates buzz and opens doors.
- Mentors love projects that are real, visible, and evolving.

Tracking Impact (So You Can Brag a Bit)

- Pick 2–3 metrics that matter—quantitative or qualitative.
- Track them consistently and share the story.
- Celebrate tiny wins to stay in motion.

Balancing It All

- Primary job first—always. But your 10% matters too.
- Communicate progress early and often.
- When feedback hits, don't flinch—adapt.

Handling Setbacks Like a Pro

- View failure as a data point, not a dead end.
- Reflect, reset, reframe.
- Keep the project—and your energy—alive.

Sharing the Story

- Document outcomes and lessons.
- Make your project visible in meetings, updates, or recaps.
- It's not showing off. It's showing value.

Using 10% Projects for Career Moves

- If you're job searching, start small and smart.
- Use projects to rebuild confidence, reconnect, and stand out.
- Show you're active, learning, and resilient.

For College Students (or Career Launchers)

- Stand out by showing initiative before you get the job.
- Choose projects that speak to your future field.
- Keep them focused, consistent, and brag-worthy.

For Kids and Teens

- Start simple: lemonade stands, newsletters, mini businesses.
- Let them lead—your job is encouragement and scaffolding.
- Focus on effort, curiosity, and confidence over outcomes.

For Retirees (or Rewired Professionals)

- Use 10% Projects to rediscover purpose, passion, or simply play.
- Choose projects that reflect your legacy, curiosity, or untapped skills.
- Focus on fulfillment, contribution, and staying mentally and socially active.

Building Your Brand Through 10% Projects

- You are your reputation—10% Projects make it visible.
- Document your growth and share the ride.
- Stay consistent with your message and mission.

Learning New Skills the 10% Project Way

- Curiosity + micro-goals = skill-building magic.
- Practice imperfectly, consistently.
- Reflect on what you're learning—not just what you've achieved.

Gaining Experience (Even When No One Asked You To)

- Experience doesn't need permission.

- Use your 10% Project to go first, try things, build stories.
- The right people will notice. Even if they're not watching yet.

Getting Comfortable With Risk

- Fear is data—not a stop sign.
- Risk is where confidence is born.
- Start before you feel ready. The clarity comes later.

Staying Light When It Gets Heavy

- Progress ≠ perfection.
- Find humor in the mess.
- Come back to why you started.

Avoiding Opportunity Killers

- Don't ghost your own project.
- Log progress, ask for feedback, show you care.
- Treat it like it matters—because it does.

Owning Your Reputation

- Ask: "How am I currently seen?" Then decide what to shift.
- Feedback is your flashlight.
- Visibility is your lever. Use it on purpose.

Networking Through 10% Projects

- Talk less about "connecting." Show what you're building.
- Share early, invite feedback, ask questions.

- People love helping people who are in motion.

Maintaining Strong Relationships

- Use your 10% Project as a conversation starter.
- Keep light contact with meaningful updates.
- Gratitude = relationship rocket fuel.

Building an Intentional Network

- Think depth over width.
- Be the one who connects others.
- Use your project as the reason to reach out.

The Mentoring Mindset

- Networking opens doors. Mentoring helps you walk through them.
- Great mentors guide, challenge, and celebrate with you.
- Use tools like your Personal Growth Map to structure the journey.

Keeping the Relationships That Matter

- Check in, even when there's no agenda.
- Keep track of the little details—people remember.
- End strong. Leave relationships better than you found them.

"Ideas without action
aren't ideas.
They're regrets."

Steve Jobs

SECTION 9
10% Projects in Real Life

CHAPTER 32

The Author's 10% Projects

The genesis of the 10% Project Book was a slide in a presentation I made to The Ohio State University MBA program. I was asked to give the students an overview of the career path that led me to a leadership role in a tech startup in Silicon Valley.

One of the charts from that presentation is included in the following pages, and illustrates the key 10% Projects that changed my life.

I have many, many more 10% projects written up in a file on my laptop, some of which I implemented, and some of which didn't go anywhere (yet ☺).

In this chapter my goal is to include case studies that provide insight into some of the 10% Projects that made a serious impact on both my career and my life.

The 10% Projects that Changed my Life

Undergraduate
Psychology

Public Relations &
Masters in Marketing

The Boeing
Leadership Center

MACQUARIE University
SYDNEY·AUSTRALIA

UTS
UNIVERSITY OF TECHNOLOGY, SYDNEY

1990's   2000's

Sydney Australia   Melbourne Aust. | St Louis

Local Govt   Agency   Subsidiary

Municipal Library

Ad Agency
MARKETING STRATEGY

Air Traffic Control Software

10% PROJECT **Children's Activities**
>PR Officer

10% PROJECT **Graphic Design**
>Boeing Position

10% PROJECT **Seattle Conference**
>Boeing Networking

Public Relations
LOVING LIVING KU-RING-GAI
Ku-ring-gai Council

Corporate Travel

10% PROJECT **Off-Set Program**
>Relocation to USA

10% PROJECT **Charity Fundraiser**
>Marketing Position

Boeing Leadership Center

10% PROJECT **Networking**
>Corporate Position

The 10% Projects that Changed my Life

Executive MBA
Northwestern University

Digital Marketing
& Social Media

Kellogg
School of Management

Berkeley
UNIVERSITY OF CALIFORNIA

2010's

Chicago | Seattle

United Kingdom | St Louis

Fortune 50 Corporation

Corporate HQ

International M&A

T-X

10% PROJECT Boeing Team Building
>Kellogg MBA

10% PROJECT Marketing Audit
> COS Role

Commercial Airplanes

Boeing Global Services

JSTARS

Space Shuttle

10% PROJECT Marketing Training
> HX Connection

10% PROJECT Venture Research
> HX Marketing

The 10% Projects that Changed my Life

**Design Thinking &
Product Management**

**Coaching | Training
& Lecturing**

Cornell University

STARTUP

2010's → 2020's

Silicon Valley, California

Corporate VC

Start-ups

BOEING HORIZONX
Corporate Venture Capital

BOEINGNEXT
New Business Ventures

Personal Air Vehicles

Cargo Air Vehicles

10% PROJECT Strategizer Training
> Start-up Support

Portfolio Support

MATTERNET

FORTEM TECHNOLOGIES

sparkcognition

UP SKILL

NEAR EARTH AUTONOMY

Robotic Skies.

C360
A VIDEO REVOLUTION

MORF3D

Unmanned Surface Vehicles

10% PROJECT Ohio State
> 10% Project Book
> Start-up Mkting Book

10% PROJECT Marketing Plan
> VP Position

Thermal Solutions

10% PROJECT 10% Project Book
>Corporate Presentations

10% PROJECT Start-up Mkting Book
>VC Sponsored
  Start-up Training

Case Study:

Turning Dull Days into Dynamic Engagement

The Situation

In Sydney, Australia, I took a year off college and decided to get a full-time job. I found work as a library assistant at the local library for Ku-ring-gai Council, Gordon Library. It was a great fit since I loved books, but there was one downside—Tuesdays were incredibly dull. The library was closed to the public, and we had to do "shelf check," which involved reorganizing misplaced books. It was monotonous and lacked the engagement I craved.

The 10% Project

I decided to take the initiative and started running after-school children's activities at Gordon Library. These activities were designed to encourage young readers and provide a creative, welcoming environment for kids after school. The response was overwhelmingly positive—parents loved the program, and the children's section of the library became more vibrant and more fun. Seeing how well the program was received, the library staff and management took notice.

The Opportunity That Arose

After witnessing the success of my self-initiated project, the children's librarian from Turramurra Library—another branch in the same network—approached me. Turramurra Library was open to the public on Tuesdays and ran a special children's program. Given how well I had handled the after-school sessions at Gordon, they asked if I would be interested in helping at Turramurra on Tuesdays. I gladly accepted the opportunity.

This shift meant I no longer had to do the dreaded shelf check. Instead, I spent my Tuesdays engaging children in storytelling and educational activities—something I genuinely enjoyed. This project not only made my work more fulfilling but also allowed me to develop skills in event planning, photography, promotions, and community engagement.

The Outcome

By proactively creating a 10% Project at Gordon Library, I demonstrated my initiative and creativity, which directly led to new opportunities at Turramurra Library. This experience also paved the way for my next job, as I had developed skills in public engagement and event coordination. In retrospect, this was one of my earliest successful 10% Projects, where taking the initiative led to professional growth, more enjoyable work, and a new career opportunity.

Case Study:

The Detour That Defined My Career

How a "pause" from university became my path forward

Context

During my undergraduate degree in Australia, I took advantage of a government program that allowed students to pause university, work for two years, and then receive financial support to return and finish their degree. It sounded practical—and at the time, I fully intended to go back and complete my early childhood education studies.

The Situation

While working as a library assistant at Ku-ring-gai Municipal Council, a role opened internally for a Public Relations Assistant. I had never formally worked in PR, but I realized that many of the things I'd been doing proactively—creating displays, running children's programs, organizing events, and speaking publicly—were closely aligned with the role. Instead of assuming I wasn't qualified, I decided to make the case that I was.

The 10% Project

I wrote up informal case studies of everything I'd done at the library and applied for the PR Assistant role. Once I got the job, I treated it as a learning platform. Alongside my day job, I enrolled in a part-time public relations course to build the technical skills I knew I'd need to grow.

That course—started while I was still an assistant—became my 10% Project. It gave me confidence, credibility, and practical tools well beyond my formal role.

The Outcome

When my manager's role later opened, I was ready. The combination of hands-on experience and proactive skill-building enabled me to step into the Public Relations Officer position. From there, one opportunity led to another—into marketing, advertising, and eventually the career I've built ever since.

Choosing momentum over my original plan to return to university turned out to be the best professional decision I ever made.

Key Takeaway

You don't always need a new degree to change direction—you need to start learning before you're asked to.

By investing in myself early, I turned a temporary role into a permanent exciting and rewarding career shift.

Case Study:

Pedaling for a Purpose

How One Ride Changed My Career

Background:

After transitioning from a library assistant role to Public Relations at Ku-ring-gai Municipal Council, I found myself in a new and exciting career path. This leap was a risk, but it was fueled by the skills I had developed during my time at the library, such as presentations, event planning, and promotional activities. I decided to embrace this new opportunity with enthusiasm.

The 10% Project:

One day, my manager mentioned that she was entering a competition that required charity fundraising. Wanting to help, I took the initiative to organize a charity bike ride from Hornsby to Gosford (a challenging four-hour ride) as a fundraising event. Given my fitness level at the time, I thought it would be a manageable and fun way to contribute. Initially, I envisioned a small group ride, but my experience from the library—promoting children's activities and designing engaging events—helped me think bigger. I promoted the event through various channels, spoke to community groups, and rallied support from council employees.

The Event:

What started as a simple idea evolved into a large-scale event called "Cycle for a Kid Who Can't," attracting 321 cyclists. Volunteers from every department of the council joined, helping with tasks such as manning drink stations, driving support vehicles, and acting as route marshals. The event became a full-fledged community effort, complete with giveaways, participant awards, and a sausage sizzle BBQ at the finish line.

Impact and Outcome:

The event raised over $20,000, a substantial amount at the time. The local council acknowledged the success with a 'Mayoral Minute', archiving my contribution as part of the council's official records. The Mayor even decreed that the event would become an annual council tradition. Beyond the immediate success, the event significantly boosted team morale, fostering collaboration among council employees and creating a positive community spirit.

The Unexpected Opportunity:

One unexpected but life-changing outcome was the career opportunity that followed. My boss's brother, who owned an advertising agency, attended the event and saw the skills I demonstrated in organizing, promoting, and mobilizing a large group. Impressed by my initiative and ability to execute the project so effectively, he offered me a position at his advertising agency—an opportunity beyond my imagination.

Key Takeaway:

This case study highlights how a small idea, when approached with passion and commitment, can turn into something remarkable. By proactively taking on a 10% Project that aligned with both my interests and community needs, I not only made a positive impact but also advanced my career in an unexpected and meaningful way.

Case Study:

From Watching to Winning

Curiosity to Career Upgrade

Context:

After transitioning from public relations to the dynamic world of advertising, I found myself working at Advertising Professionals, a medium-sized comprehensive agency specializing in advertising, marketing, and incentive planning. The agency had a diverse client base ranging from large companies like H&R Block, Fort Dodge, Elna Sewing Machines, and Faberge to smaller businesses, including a financial investment newsletter publisher, a conference planning company, and skincare product manufacturers.

The Situation:

One of my early tasks involved creating layouts for advertisements. At the time, graphic design and typesetting programs were just starting to take off, and the process typically involved writing the copy creating detailed layout, and then going to professional designers who used Apple computers and software like QuarkXPress, Illustrator, and Photoshop. I would stand behind them, watching closely as they assembled the layouts I had conceptualized.

The 10% Project:

After observing the designers for some time, I realized that the process didn't look as complicated as I initially thought. I became convinced that with the right tools and a bit of self-directed learning, I could manage the typesetting and graphic design tasks in-house. I approached the agency's managing director and proposed that if he invested in an Apple computer and the necessary software, I would teach myself the skills required to take over the design work. He agreed, seeing the potential cost savings and efficiency improvements. I dedicated a portion of my time to learning the software and experimenting with design. As I became more proficient, I started handling all the agency's design and layout tasks entirely on my own. This significantly reduced outsourcing costs and expedited the turnaround time since I no longer needed to explain my vision to external designers.

The Outcome:

Over the next decade at the agency, I continued to take on similar 10% Projects that expanded my skill set and increased my responsibilities. My proactive approach and ability to streamline design processes ultimately led to me becoming the manager of the agency. Even in that leadership role, I continued to leverage my hands-on graphic design skills, maintaining a deep connection with the creative side of advertising. This experience and the versatile skill set I developed paved the way for my next career move as Marketing Director at a subsidiary of The Boeing Company.

Key Takeaway:

Sometimes, all it takes is a willingness to learn and a proactive mindset to turn a perceived challenge into a career-defining opportunity. By combining creativity with technical skills, I not only improved the agency's efficiency but also positioned myself as a more versatile and valuable asset to the team.

Case Study:

Trading Tourist Attractions for Career Traction

Context

While working as Marketing Director at Preston Aviation Solutions, a subsidiary of The Boeing Company, I organized a global user group meeting in Seattle, an annual product-focused offsite event. The event ran from Monday to Thursday, leaving Friday open for personal time before we flew back to Australia.

The Situation

While my colleagues chose to explore Seattle on the day off, I saw an opportunity to build professional connections. I had been in touch with Dawn, the Operations Director at Boeing Commercial Airplanes, and decided to spend my free day meeting with her instead of sightseeing. I visited Boeing's headquarters and had a productive meeting with Dawn, during which I shared my aspirations to work more closely with Boeing - our parent company.

The 10% Project

By proactively networking, I strengthened my relationship with Dawn, who then offered to help me set up meetings with various regional sales directors in Boeing Commercial Airplanes. This was a rare opportunity, as gaining access to these decision-makers was typically challenging.

The Outcome

I flew back to Seattle within a few weeks, as the subsidiary approved my return for these high-impact meetings. Dawn's support enabled me to present our software solution to the regional sales teams, highlighting its value and customer benefits. My presentations were well-received, and the exposure significantly boosted my profile within Boeing. This led to increased sales for the product and, just as significantly, an invitation for me to attend Boeing's prestigious Leadership Development Program at their Leadership Center—a once-in-a-lifetime professional growth experience.

Key Takeaway

Taking the initiative to foster meaningful professional relationships, even when it means sacrificing leisure time, can result in career-changing opportunities. By leveraging a small window of time strategically, I opened doors that propelled my career forward within one of the world's largest aerospace companies.

Case Study:

Offsetting Challenges:

Turning a Bold Idea into a Leadership Leap

Context

One of the most significant 10% Projects I undertook led to a major career transformation—relocating from Melbourne, Australia, to St. Louis, Missouri, to work at the Boeing Leadership Center. This iconic facility could house close to 300 employees and ran a range of leadership and functional excellence programs. My journey to this pivotal role began with a single innovative idea.

The Situation

At the time, I was working as the Marketing Director at Preston Aviation Solutions, a subsidiary of Boeing based in Melbourne. One day, I came across an email discussing offset programs. In the context of defense sales, Boeing would commit to investing in the purchasing country's economy—in this case, Australia—when they made a substantial sale, such as the 767 tanker. The idea was to foster business growth and technology advancement in the purchasing country.

I realized that our Australian-based subsidiary, which primarily developed software for commercial airspace, could potentially benefit from this offset funding if we developed a new product for defense airspace. It struck me that Boeing investing in our Australian subsidiary would not only support local technology but also meet Australia's preference for increasing technological expertise and promoting exports, given that 90% of our sales were international.

The 10% Project

I decided to explore this concept further, despite it not being directly related to my core responsibilities. I researched offset programs, the rules surrounding investment credits, and how they could be applied to our subsidiary. I also evaluated the benefits from Australia's perspective, including increased technological capability, job creation, and export potential.

I documented my proposal thoroughly, presenting it to the CEO at Preston Aviation Solutions. He was impressed and encouraged me to take it further. This led to a series of presentations to various Boeing divisions, including Boeing Defense Systems, the offset organization in Washington, D.C., the warfighter team, and finally, the manufacturing team responsible for the 767 tanker. Aligning all these groups was a massive undertaking, requiring me to incorporate feedback, refine my proposal, and build consensus.

The Outcome

Although the 767 Tanker sale to Australia was eventually put on hold for reasons beyond my control, the 10% Project itself was transformative for me personally. The process of aligning multiple stakeholders and navigating complex corporate structures significantly raised my profile within Boeing. I developed a robust international network and honed my project management, planning, communication, and strategic thinking skills.

The lasting impact was profound. Even though the project did not come to fruition, my proactive approach and ability to mobilize support across the organization was recognized.

These efforts were a key factor when the Boeing Leadership Center offered me a life-changing opportunity to relocate to the U.S. and teach leadership and marketing to Boeing Executives and emerging leaders.

This move from the Australia to the US, and embarking on a completely new career, marked a major turning point in my life.

Key Takeaway

Sometimes, the journey itself matters more than the outcome. Pursuing a challenging project, even when the final result is uncertain, can build invaluable skills, connections, and opportunities. A 10% Project that pushes your boundaries and expands your network can be life-changing—even if it doesn't pan out as planned.

Case Study:

The Project that Opened the Boardroom Door

How Networking Changed my Career

Context

While working at the Boeing Leadership Center (the BLC), a state-of-the-art facility designed to enhance leadership skills and foster networking across the global Boeing organization, I had the opportunity to observe the incredible power of building connections. The BLC hosted leaders and high-potential employees from all over the Boeing Company, which employed around 150,000 people at the time. As a Senior Program Manager, I was responsible for organizing leadership and professional development programs.

The Situation

Toward the end of my first year at the BLC, I learned of a senior manager position opening at Boeing's Corporate World Headquarters in Chicago. The role involved working with the Board of Directors and the Executive Council to coordinate meetings, events, strategic reviews, and managing various high-stakes organizational tasks. It sounded like an exciting next step, but I knew competition would be tough

The 10% Project

During my time at the BLC, I had made a conscious effort to build and maintain relationships with people from different parts of the company. I stayed at the Center during evenings to participate in networking events, social activities, and informal gatherings. Over the year, I developed a strong network of colleagues who knew my work and respected my commitment.

When I heard about the position in Chicago, I reached out to my network to get advice and guidance. I spoke with several colleagues who offered insights and encouragement. Unbeknownst to me at the time, some of them proactively reached out to the hiring manager in Chicago and recommended me for the role. Their support proved invaluable. When I was invited for the interview, I felt confident because I knew I had advocates who believed in my abilities.

The Outcome

I got the position. Moving from the BLC to the Corporate World Headquarters in Chicago was a career-defining step. Reflecting on this experience, I realized how crucial that intentional networking had been. Interestingly, a friend and colleague at the BLC, who had similar qualifications and tenure, expressed surprise that I had secured such a significant opportunity. The difference lay in the relationships I had built. While she focused solely on her immediate work and day-to-day execution, I had been doing the same but had also been actively engaging with colleagues and forming professional connections.

This experience taught me that networking is not just about collecting contacts, but about being genuinely interested in people, investing time to build relationships, and being consistent in maintaining those connections.

Key Takeaway

Intentional networking can dramatically impact your career path. By staying curious, being approachable, and actively engaging with peers, I not only advanced my career but also demonstrated the value of building professional relationships in a way that goes beyond mere acquaintance.

Case Study:

From River Race to MBA

How a River Race Became My Fast Track to an Executive MBA

Context

While working as Senior Manager at Boeing's Corporate World Headquarters in Chicago, I faced a challenge: I was new to the area and, having relocated from Australia the year before, knew very few people. I wanted to integrate into the community and build connections. Fortunately, Boeing had a community engagement program, which included various volunteer and charity events.

The Situation

One of the major annual events was the Corporate River Race, where local corporations would enter a whaling boat, with a team of nine—eight paddlers and one caller—to compete in a race on the Chicago River. The event raised funds to help clean up the river, and Boeing had traditionally participated.

The 10% Project

Eager to make an impact and build relationships, I volunteered to take over the organization of Boeing's participation in the race. Instead of just forming a single team, I proposed an innovative 10% Project - a longitudinal experiential team-building program - that would involve as many departments as possible over the three months leading up to the race.

The program included weekly "Lunch and Learn" events focusing on health, fitness, leadership development, and team training. Participants practiced rowing techniques, discussed healthy eating habits, and participated in leadership discussions. The initiative created massive enthusiasm, with 131 Boeing employees forming multiple teams, each with their own team names, custom t-shirts, and team pride.

The Outcome

On race day, more than 90% of Boeing's Corporate Headquarter employees turned out to support their colleagues. The teams, proudly wearing their customized shirts, rowed in the event while their families and coworkers cheered from the riverbanks. The initiative not only raised significant funds for the Chicago River cleanup, but also significantly boosted engagement, morale and camaraderie among employees. The event garnered local media attention, further elevating Boeing's community presence.

The Impact

My proactive leadership and successful coordination of this large-scale event raised my visibility within Boeing, particularly at the executive level. As a direct result, Boeing sponsored me for an executive MBA program at the Kellogg School of Management at Northwestern University—an incredible opportunity that significantly shaped my future career trajectory.

Key Takeaway

Sometimes a small initiative can grow into something transformative. By fostering community engagement, I not only strengthened employee relationships but also positioned myself as a proactive leader, ultimately unlocking new career opportunities.

Case Study:

From Terror to Teaching

Context

When I started my Executive MBA at Kellogg (Northwestern University), I was excited—but also nervous. I'm not really a "numbers person" and while I enjoy building spreadsheets, finance had never been my strength. Very quickly, that fear turned into real doubt about whether I belonged in the program at all.

The Situation

The finance coursework was overwhelming, and I seriously considered dropping out. The concepts didn't come naturally, and no amount of late-night rereading was helping things click. I knew that if I didn't find a different way to learn, I wouldn't survive the program—let alone succeed.

The 10% Project

Instead of quitting, a friend and I arranged regular tutoring sessions with a PhD student who was supporting the class.

To reinforce what I was learning, I built detailed spreadsheets for every finance topic—NPV, valuations, and core financial models—embedding all the formulas so the logic became visible and repeatable.

What started as a personal learning tool quickly spread. I shared the spreadsheets with classmates, then more people asked for them, and soon I was running informal lunchtime sessions teaching others how to use them. Because the program wasn't graded on a curve, there was no downside to sharing—and teaching the material helped cement it for me.

Outcome

The results were dramatic. I went from nearly dropping out to scoring 100% on every finance exam. My classmates continued using the spreadsheets for years, and even the Kellogg program leaders thanked me for stepping up and modeling collaborative leadership.

Later, when I applied for a mergers and acquisitions role at Boeing—where financial fluency was essential—I used this experience as proof that I could master unfamiliar skills quickly and deeply. I got the role, and it became a pivotal step in my career.

Key Takeaway

A 10% Project can turn your biggest weakness into evidence of your strength. By finding a new way to learn—and then sharing it—I transformed a subject I feared into a capability that opened new doors.

Case Study:

The Bold Pitch

How Challenging the Status Quo Led to My Big Break

Context

After leaving Boeing World Headquarters in Chicago, I moved back to St. Louis to join the Global Services and Support International M&A team at Boeing Defense. My primary role focused on increasing the strategic global footprint in Australia and the UK. Although I secured the position primarily due to my recently earned Executive MBA, I had no prior M&A experience. Nonetheless, I embraced the opportunity and quickly immersed myself in the new responsibilities.

The Situation

While participating in new business proposals, bids, and responses to RFPs (requests for proposals), I noticed an opportunity to apply more marketing principles to the process.

My extensive marketing background made me recognize that a more market-driven approach could improve customer engagement, enhance proposal quality, and ultimately increase our win rates.

The 10% Project

My idea was to conduct an analysis of the sales, wins, and losses to identify trends and gaps. I also conducted interviews with various stakeholders to gather insights. My goal was to present a strategy that applied market focused thinking to business development processes. I compiled my findings into a detailed presentation deck, complete with analysis and proposed improvements.

Once the analysis was ready, I actively sought out feedback from leadership. I scheduled meetings with senior executives in business development, the defense business, and other key stakeholders. This was a bold move since I was engaging directly with senior VPs and divisional heads. I even created a matrix to track feedback, mapping out who supported the ideas and who needed more convincing.

One significant interaction was with Dennis Muilenburg, then President of Global Services and Support. I presented my ideas to him and candidly asked for feedback, expressing a willingness to adjust my approach based on his input. His supportive response encouraged me to continue presenting the concept to others.

The Outcome

While it is hard to measure the direct impact of my initiative on Boeing's marketing practices, the project significantly elevated my visibility within the company. My proactive approach and willingness to challenge existing practices left a positive impression on many senior leaders. Ultimately, when a position opened as Chief of Staff for Dennis Muilenburg, I applied and was selected. This role gave me incredible exposure across Boeing's business divisions, exposing me to diverse leadership challenges and further expanding my experience and network.

Key Takeaway

This 10% Project highlights the importance of proactively identifying gaps and proposing solutions, even when it means stepping out of your comfort zone. By taking ownership of a challenge, I not only gained invaluable experience, but also positioned myself for a career-defining role working closely with one of Boeing's best and most influential leaders.

Case Study:

Learning, Leading, and Landing the Next Big Role

Context

I joined Boeing Horizon X, the Corporate Venture Capital division of The Boeing Company, in early 2018 thanks to the strong support from Boeing Executives Logan Jones, Steve Nordlund, and Dennis Muilenburg.

I had built relationships with these leaders over the years, which made the move possible. Around the same time, Boeing established Boeing Next, a new ventures organization focused on rapid market entry for new products and capabilities, including eVTOL autonomous cargo and personal air vehicles. My role involved marketing for both Boeing Next and Boeing Horizon X, supporting various initiatives and new business ventures.

The Situation

One of my early challenges was identifying tools to help us better understand how to bring business opportunities to market. I discovered the Strategizer tools—particularly the Value Proposition Canvas and the Business Model Canvas. These tools are designed to simplify the complex process of building business models and crafting value propositions in a way that resonates with customers.

The 10% Project

I proposed attending a Strategizer course to deepen my understanding of these tools and how they could benefit both Boeing Horizon X and its portfolio companies. After attending the week-long training in Boston with four colleagues, I returned inspired to implement what I had learned. I initiated a series of training programs for both internal teams and portfolio companies, presenting the Strategizer concepts to leadership and providing hands-on workshops in our Menlo Park offices.

This proactive approach led to an expansion of my role, as I began consulting directly with leadership teams from portfolio companies, guiding them through creating their own business model and value proposition canvases. This project significantly increased experience with Startups and my visibility and scope within Boeing.

Outcome

The skills I developed through this 10% Project had long-lasting benefits. Later, when applying for a role at a startup called Saildrone, I presented my resume alongside a value proposition canvas that highlighted how I could personally bring value to the company. This unique approach made me stand out and helped me to secure the job—despite the challenge of transitioning from a large corporate environment like Boeing to a small scrappy startup.

Key Takeaway

By proactively identifying useful tools and sharing the knowledge gained with the broader team, I not only expanded my own skills, but also increased my professional visibility. This project exemplifies how leveraging new methods and taking calculated risks can open unexpected doors.

Case Study:

From Skill Gap to Superpower

How an 8-hour course changed my career trajectory

Context

After nearly 20 years at Boeing, I began seriously considering a move from a large corporate environment into smaller startups. As I assessed my skills honestly, I realized there was one glaring gap: I didn't have hands-on media pitching experience. In a startup, I knew I wouldn't be able to rely on specialists—I'd need to do much more myself.

The Situation

I wanted to be credible and confident when interviewing for startup roles, but media relations felt like a weak spot. I knew I couldn't just say, "I'll figure it out later." If I was going to make this transition, I needed to close that gap quickly and deliberately.

The 10% Project

Before I even started interviewing, I searched online for ways to build practical media skills and found an eight-hour training course from 'Muck Rack', a media management tool, on pitching journalists. I sat down and watched the entire program, taking detailed notes and treating it like a real investment in my future.

When it came time to send my first media pitch, I followed the approach from the training almost word for word. It worked. From there, I practiced, refined, and personalized the method until media pitching became second nature.

Outcome

What started as an eight-hour self-directed learning project became one of my strongest professional assets. Five years after leaving Boeing, media relations is now one of the biggest value-adds I bring to any company.

In the last 3 years alone, I've helped generate nearly 4,000 earned media articles, reaching over 15 billion people worldwide, with an estimated earned media value of more than $140 million—all stemming from a single weekend spent closing a skill gap

Key Takeaway

Sometimes a 10% Project isn't about doing more work—it's about fixing one critical weakness. By investing a small amount of focused time to build a missing skill, I turned a gap into a defining strength that reshaped my career.

Case Study:

The 10% Project Book

The Day I Realized My Career Strategy Was Worth a Book

THE GENESIS OF THE 10% PROJECT CONCEPT

Context

After leaving the security of a large corporation and transitioning to a startup in Silicon Valley, I joined Saildrone, a company known for its innovative unmanned surface vehicles (USVs), that collect environmental and maritime marine data. While working there, I continued to take on numerous 10% Projects to expand my impact.

The Situation

One day, a mentor, Ken Colman, asked me to speak to a group of MBA students from The Ohio State University. These students visited Silicon Valley to learn about startup culture and innovation. Ken thought they would find my career transition from a large corporation to a startup particularly insightful.

The 10% Project

I took on the challenge of crafting a presentation about my career journey, including how taking on additional projects played a critical role in unlocking key opportunities throughout my career. While preparing the presentation,

I realized that these small, proactive initiatives were the true catalysts for my major career milestones. I called them my 10% Projects. Projects that were done on the edges of my day job in addition to my primary work statement.

During the session, I explained how I consistently used 10% Projects to build skills, gain visibility, and create opportunities. One of the MBA students, Liz, approached me afterward, suggesting that I write a book on the 10% Project concept. Of course, as a leader in an intense startup environment, and the parent of a very active 12 year old, I didn't have a lot of spare time - the excuse I always used for not undertaking things I wanted to do for myself – in this case write a book. However, Liz's enthusiasm, combined with other students' positive reactions, sparked the idea to make writing a book about the 10% Project a 10% Project in itself.

Outcome

Inspired by this feedback, I made the commitment to write "The 10% Project" book as my next 10% Project. This was a pivotal moment that transformed a career insight into a structured methodology aimed at helping others achieve personal and professional growth.

Key Takeaway

Sometimes the best ideas come from sharing your story and listening to feedback. By presenting my career path and the importance of small proactive projects, I discovered the potential to formalize the 10% Project concept and share it on a scale that has already exceeded my wildest expectations.

Case Study:

Pitch Perfect

How a 10% Project Secured My Dream Job

Context

While working at Saildrone, I had been with the company for about two years, when I was approached by a headhunter about an exciting opportunity. The role was Vice President of Marketing at a startup that was still in stealth mode, but planned to make a significant market debut. The company, Frore Systems, focused on solid-state active cooling—a revolutionary way of cooling electronics. Initially, I was hesitant as the industry was entirely new to me—thermal, electronics, and computer components were not my areas of expertise. However, after speaking with the CEO and realizing the potential impact of the technology, I decided that this was an opportunity worth pursuing.

The Situation

The final step in the interview process was a presentation to the leadership team. Knowing how crucial this was, I decided to take it on as a short-term 10% Project, even though it meant dedicating almost two full weekends to preparing the pitch. I created a comprehensive marketing plan that went beyond their expectations. It included recommendations on naming, branding, and positioning, ad copy, market segmentation, value propositions, and persona canvases. The goal was to showcase not just ideas, but a complete strategic vision for bringing the product to market.

The 10% Project

My dedication paid off. I treated the preparation like a full-fledged marketing project, going well beyond what most would do for a job interview. When I delivered the presentation, I handed them the entire plan on a memory stick, emphasizing that they could use it regardless of whether they hired me. The CEO appreciated the depth of my thinking and the effort I put in, and ultimately, I was offered the job. The CEO, Seshu, valued my ability to approach the problem differently and saw potential in bringing a fresh perspective to the industry.

Outcome

Accepting the role required a massive learning curve as I had no background in engineering, thermal management, or computer hardware. Fortunately, I love learning, love a challenge, and the CEO was incredibly supportive. This new role at Frore Systems positioned me within a cutting-edge startup that is poised to make a generational change in the electronics industry. By applying the 10% Project mindset to the interview process itself, I secured a role that challenged me and promised significant long-term rewards.

Key Takeaway

Sometimes a 10% Project is about seizing a moment to go above and beyond, even when the odds seem daunting. Putting in the extra effort during the interview process made me stand out and demonstrated my commitment and strategic thinking. It also reinforced the principle that taking calculated risks and dedicating focused effort can yield remarkable career breakthroughs.

Case Study:

From Gabby's Mom to Guest Speaker

HOW ONE CONVERSATION SPARKED AN IMPORTANT OPPORTUNITY

Context

As I was writing the 10% Project book, I found myself sharing the concept with people I encountered in everyday life. One day, while dropping off my daughter, Gabby, at her friend Safi's house, I got into a conversation with Safie's mother, Tracy. I shared the concept of the book and how I was having fun creating it. Tracy found the idea of the 10% project intriguing, especially since she had done similar things but never intentionally as a strategic career development strategy.

The Situation

A few weeks later, Tracy mentioned that she had talked about the 10% Project concept at work. She had discussed it with her Manager at a major software company, who thought it was exactly the kind of mindset change they needed. Tracy then suggested that I come and present the concept to their team. Presenting at a company with a reputation like this particular software company was an incredible opportunity. It also made me realize how sharing my passion projects can organically lead to new prospects.

The 10% Project

Writing the book itself became a 10% Project, including proactively sharing the concept with people I knew. This openness led to Tracy seeing me not just as "Gabby's mom" but as someone with valuable ideas worth sharing.

Outcome

The presentation went extremely well and I am now in discussions with them and a leading Silicon Valley University, to implement and study a 12-week program with to measure the impact of the 10% Project on Employee Satisfaction, Engagement and Confidence in the Workplace. This opportunity and associated academic study could add significant credibility to the 10% Project concept and would be a major milestone in building a new career in public speaking—something I envision doing more of in the future, particularly post-retirement from the Silicon Valley Start-up world.

Key Takeaway

Sometimes, casually sharing what you're working on can open doors you never expected. By being open about my passion for the concept of 10% Projects, I positioned myself for a potentially game-changing opportunity.

CHAPTER 33

Case studies by Group

10% Projects Work for Everyone — Here's the Proof.

Big goals are great. But real growth? It often starts small — with one spark, one question, one bold little step. These case studies are here to show you just how powerful that step can be.

In the following pages, you'll find real-world examples of people who used 10% Projects to explore a curiosity, build a bridge, reignite momentum, or completely reshape what they thought was possible.

No matter the age or stage, a 10% Project gave them permission to try, grow, and rediscover their potential.

As you read:

- If you're working in a job that feels too small — see what happens when you start treating a passion seriously.
- If you're at home balancing life and family — find purpose in the quiet pockets of time.
- If you're between jobs or rebuilding — let a small project remind you what you're capable of.
- If you're just starting out or reinventing yourself — you don't have to wait for permission to start.
- And if you're retired or resetting — your talents are still valuable, and your impact still matters.

These aren't just stories. They're possibilities.
And maybe, just maybe, one of them will spark an idea of your own.

Retail Career Case Study: Discovering a Hidden Talent on the Job

The Context

Samantha had been working at a local retail clothing store for a few years. Like many retail jobs, her days were filled with folding clothes, ringing up customers, and managing the occasional messy fitting room. But there was one part of the job she secretly loved: creating eye-catching displays.

Whether it was styling mannequins, arranging signage, or setting up window features, she found herself getting completely absorbed in the creative process. And it showed. Customers often commented on how fresh and inviting the store looked—and her manager noticed too.

The Situation

One day, Sam's boss asked if she'd like to take over all the store's visual merchandising. It wasn't part of her job description, but she jumped at the chance. It gave her a creative outlet, made work more fulfilling, and turned an ordinary job into something she felt proud of.

Even though she had no formal training, she started watching YouTube videos on visual merchandising, browsing Pinterest for inspiration, and studying how major brands set up their store layouts.

That spark led to a simple question:

"What would happen if I actually got serious about this?"

The 10% Project

Sam decided to enroll in a part-time retail design course at her local community college. She juggled work and classes, using the skills she was learning to enhance her store displays even further. Her before-and-after photos became her portfolio.

After a few months, she applied for a junior visual merchandiser role at a large national retailer. Thanks to her real-world experience, creative instincts, and fresh training, she got the job.

Outcome

Today, Sam is working full-time on a regional visual merchandising team, traveling between stores to design product displays, guide store launches, and even consult on brand aesthetics. What started as an unnoticed strength in a minimum-wage job turned into a vibrant and unexpected career path.

Key Takeaway

- Sometimes your talent is hiding in the parts of your job you love most.
- You don't need permission to start treating something seriously.

A 10% Project can turn "just a job" into the first step of a calling.

Tech Career Case Study

From Curiosity to Co-Founder

The Context

Patrick had always been known as a "code guy." For over a decade, he'd built a successful career in software engineering—writing clean code, fixing bugs, and mentoring junior developers. But quietly, he felt something shifting.

He was still great at his job, but a new curiosity was tugging at him—something he hadn't felt since his early days in tech. It wasn't just about how software worked... it was about what software could build.

He found himself more and more drawn to the business side of tech: product development, strategy, innovation. He wanted to understand not just the code behind the product— but the *why*, the *who*, and the *what's next*.

The Situation

Patrick didn't want to leave coding behind entirely, but he knew he wanted to grow. So he asked himself:

"What area of tech do I want to get smarter in?"
"Where is there momentum I could catch early?"

His answer: **blockchain**. It was complex, evolving fast, and full of potential for both coders and business thinkers. It felt like the perfect blend of challenge and opportunity.

The 10% Project

Patrick started small. He set aside just a few hours a week to study blockchain architecture, smart contracts, and token ecosystems. He signed up for online classes, contributed to open-source projects, and even built a few sample applications to test his skills.

As his confidence grew, he applied for a part-time consulting role with a small startup building blockchain-enabled supply chain software. That gig turned into a full-time position, where Patrick expanded beyond code—helping with product direction, customer insights, and business strategy.

Then came the big break.

Through an advanced blockchain development course, Patrick was introduced to two founders with a big vision and a need for a technical co-founder. They invited him to join their startup. Patrick said yes.

Outcome

Today, Patrick is a co-founder of a growing Web3 company, combining his deep technical roots with a new passion for business-building.

He didn't abandon his identity as a coder.
He expanded it—one small bold step at a time.

Key Takeaways

- A 10% Project can help you test-drive a new field before making a leap.
- Small, consistent effort can open unexpected doors.

  You don't need permission to start learning in the direction of your curiosity.

Home Case Study

Growing a Greener Mindset at Home

One Mom's 10% Project that Blossomed into Something Bigger

Context

Emma, a full-time mom of two young kids (ages 6 and 8), wanted to create more meaningful time with her children — something beyond screen time or rushed routines. She also felt a growing concern about the environment and how disconnected her kids were from where their food actually came from.

Instead of lecturing about recycling or climate change, Emma decided to *show* them what caring for the planet could look like — in their own backyard.

The 10% Project

Emma launched a small, hands-on 10% Project at home: building a backyard vegetable garden. Not just for fun — but as a way to connect family time with purpose.

She involved her kids from the very beginning:

- They designed the layout together.
- Dug the beds, chose the vegetables, and planted seeds.

- Researched which plants would attract butterflies and pollinators.
- Tracked plant growth and learned about composting, soil health, and water conservation.

The garden quickly became a beloved family ritual. It wasn't just about vegetables — it became a space for questions, curiosity, and connection. The kids even gave the butterflies names.

Beyond the Backyard

Inspired by their home garden, Emma's kids asked to do a show-and-tell at school. That turned into a full-on classroom project on sustainability. Emma helped the teacher plan a pollinator-friendly garden at school — and ended up volunteering to lead it.

Before long, other families joined in. Emma had unintentionally become a sustainability advocate — all from one small project that started with tiny hands in the dirt.

Outcome

- Her kids now understand food systems, environmental care, and where broccoli *actually* comes from.
- The school created a new garden space with parent and teacher support.
- Emma found a new sense of purpose — blending family, values, and impact.

Key Takeaway

You don't need a big platform to make a big difference.

One garden, one family, one 10% Project — can grow into something powerful.

Job Seeker Case Study

Rebuilding Confidence & Career Momentum

The Context

After more than a decade as a full-time mom and homemaker, **Lisa** found herself at a crossroads. Her kids were getting older, the house was quieter, and for the first time in years, she had space to think about *what's next* — not just for her family, but for *her*.

She used to work in marketing, but everything in the field had changed — new platforms, new tools, new lingo. She felt behind, and truthfully, a little unsure of where to even begin.

The Situation

Lisa didn't want to jump into a full-time job right away. She wasn't sure what she wanted, and she still wanted flexibility for her family. But she also didn't want to stay stuck in "I used to..."

So she asked herself:

"What small project could I take on that would help me test the waters?"

The 10% Project

Lisa reached out to a local nonprofit that was struggling with their social media presence. She offered to help them redesign their Instagram and email newsletters in exchange for some updated experience on her resume.

She gave it a few hours each week, took free online tutorials, and slowly started rebuilding her confidence. Along the way, she realized two things:

- She still *loved* storytelling and content creation.
- She was way more tech-savvy than she'd given herself credit for.

She treated her 10% Project like a mini-apprenticeship — showing up with curiosity, learning by doing, and tracking her wins. She even started a portfolio site with examples of her work.

Outcome

Three months later, a friend forwarded her a job posting for a part-time marketing role at a small design firm. Lisa applied, shared her new project experience, and — not only did she get the job — she negotiated a flexible schedule that worked around her family life.

In under six months, she had:

- A revitalized resume.
- A strong part-time role.
- And a newfound belief in herself as a *professional*, not 'just' a parent.

Key Takeaway

- A 10% Project can be a low-risk way to *reclaim your voice and rebuild momentum.*
- You don't need a degree refresh — you need a small *spark* to prove what you still have inside.
- Confidence grows through *action*, not waiting.

College Case Study

Launching a Dream Career Through a 10% Project

Context

While leading a marketing team at Boeing, I was looking to recruit a new content creator who could bring strong digital strategy skills to the table. After posting the role, I received hundreds of applications from candidates with polished resumes and impressive degrees.

Among them was Michael — a fresh college graduate with a degree in Telecommunications. On the surface, it wasn't an obvious fit for a marketing position. In fact, when I first saw "Telecommunications," I half-wondered if it had more to do with phone systems than digital strategy.

But what made Michael stand out wasn't his degree — it was a line in his resume that said he had spent four years building his own company: **Ladybug Media Group**.

The Situation

While still a full-time student, Michael had launched and managed his own startup, where he created digital marketing strategies, produced video, designed websites, managed client relationships, and built branding campaigns for real businesses.

That experience showed me something critical: Michael didn't just learn theory — *he lived it.*

He had real-world experience solving problems, creating content, and delivering results — exactly what I needed.

When we spoke on the phone, his passion for design (and aerospace!) was obvious. He wasn't just reciting prepared answers; he was sharing real stories about building, adapting, and learning along the way.

The 10% Project

Without knowing it, Michael had been running a 10% Project for four years. Instead of waiting for graduation to start gaining experience, he created opportunities for himself while still in school. His side business taught him the exact skills and mindsets that made him not just a qualified candidate, but an outstanding one.

It was that 10% spirit — the ability to create, adapt, and lead before being formally "invited" — that convinced me to bring him in for an in-person interview.

Because of the depth of experience, he had built through his 10% Project:

- He stood out immediately.
- He earned a significantly higher starting salary than he had expected.
- And he landed his dream role at one of the most celebrated aerospace companies in the world.

Outcome

Michael's 10% Project jumpstarted his career trajectory. Today, he's thriving in the aerospace industry collaborating directly with senior executives at Fortune 50 Company. Michael's in a job he loves, one that blends his passion for marketing strategy and design with his fascination for innovation and his love of aerospace — all because he chose to start building experience before anyone asked him to.

What he built outside the classroom opened doors that a degree alone never could.

Key Takeaway

- You don't have to wait for permission to start building your future.
- Small projects, started early, often create the biggest opportunities.
- A 10% Project can be the bridge between where you are and where you dream of going.

Kid's Case Study

Turning Curiosity into a New Passion

Context

Gabby is a very special 12-year-old (my daughter) who has always loved acting. Since she was five, she had thrown herself into roles, lines, and characters — but she wanted to up her game. She realized that if she could improve her posture, movement, and presence on stage, it might help her become a stronger performer.

The Situation

Gabby decided to stretch herself by enrolling in a ballet class — even though she was starting "late" and worried she might end up surrounded by much younger kids. We were hesitant at first, unsure if there was even a class that would fit her unique goals. But through a lucky connection (and a bit of networking!), we discovered a dance class designed specifically for teens in sports, gymnastics, or performing arts — and it was a perfect match.

The 10% Project

Instead of spending her free time scrolling online or waiting for her next acting class, Gabby chose to devote a few hours each week to this new skill. What started as a small experiment to improve her acting unexpectedly unlocked a whole new passion: Ballet.

Through the class, she also met other actors, which expanded her creative community and led to new opportunities. But more surprisingly, Gabby realized she really *loved* ballet. Six months later, she had caught up to students who had been dancing for years — and was preparing to go en pointe. She now performs on stage as both an actor *and* a dancer, and spends hours at the dance studio simply because she loves it.

Outcome

Gabby's simple decision to explore something new led to:

- A second creative passion she never expected.
- New friendships and acting opportunities.
- A sense of discipline and joy that now shapes her identity.

Key Takeaway

- You're never too young (or too late) to start something new – even at 12 years old ☺.
- A 10% Project can reveal skills and passions you didn't know you had.
- What begins as support for one dream might just become a second one.

Retiree Case Study

Reigniting Purpose After Retirement

Context

Frank had recently retired from a 35-year career in engineering. At first, he enjoyed the freedom — sleeping in, long breakfasts, and catching up on books. But after a few months, the novelty wore off, and the days started to feel a little... empty.

He missed solving problems. He missed using his mind. He missed the structure. Most of all, he missed feeling *useful.*

The Situation

Frank didn't want to go back to full-time work, but he also didn't want to sit around waiting for the next golf game. So he asked himself a simple question:

"What do I still get excited about?"

His answer? *Fixing things.* He loved tinkering, troubleshooting, and making systems better.

The 10% Project

Frank decided to start a small 10% Project helping neighbors and nonprofits with basic home tech fixes — organizing messy wiring, setting up printers, improving

Wi-Fi setups, and even retrofitting old lamps with smart bulbs. He did it for free, just to stay sharp and be helpful.

Over time, word spread. He started volunteering at a local seniors center, where he not only helped people with tech issues — he also taught free workshops on "keeping up with technology" and reducing digital stress.

What began as a few hours a week turned into a fulfilling routine. He met new people, mentored younger volunteers, and felt reconnected with the world in a new way.

Outcome

Frank's 10% Project gave him:

- A renewed sense of purpose and contribution.
- Social connection and community.
- A way to blend his skills with service — on *his* terms.

Key Takeaway

- Retirement isn't the end of growth — it's the start of new possibilities.
- A small, skill-based project can reignite confidence and purpose.
- The desire to be useful never retires — it just needs a new outlet.

"A good tool improves the way you work. A great tool improves the way you think."

Jeff Duntemann

SECTION 10
Appendix

APPENDIX 1

Additional 10% Project Tools

You don't need anything more than this book to kick off your own 10% Project - it includes a step-by-step approach designed to make it easy to get started.

However, sometimes a little extra motivation or structure can help... if that's you, there are plenty of resources available to help you on your 10% Project journey at www.10percentproject.com.

The 10% Project Community

The 10% Project community is a group of motivated individuals who are always striving to add value, new ideas, insights, thoughts and advice for other '**10 Percent-ers**'. Visit the 10% Project website at www.10PercentProject.com to:

- Send us your own ideas and insight
- See all the latest ideas and advice from the 10% Project team
- Catch up on input, case studies and examples of successful 10% Projects we receive from other readers like you.
- Share your 10% Project journey—post your ideas, goals, or wins on social media!
  Use the hashtag **#My10Percent** and tag us **@My10PercentProject** so we can cheer you on!

We look forward to hearing from you!
Start small. Dream big. Make it happen.

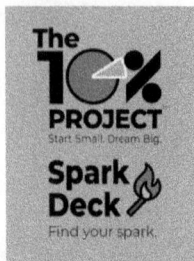

The 10% Project Spark Deck

Find your spark. Start something meaningful.

The Spark Deck is a playful, powerful tool to help you discover what energizes you — and turn it into action. Sort, reflect, and unlock patterns using the Spark Cards — to find projects with purpose.

Whether you're feeling stuck, curious, or ready to grow, your next bold step starts here.

Inside the deck:

- 70+ Spark Cards with Prompts
- 7 Spark Zones that reveal what lights you up
- A guide sheet inspired by The 10% Project™ framework

Start small. Dream big.
And let your spark lead the way.

THE 10% PROJECT

Spark
Seeker
Find your spark.

Start Small. Dream Big.

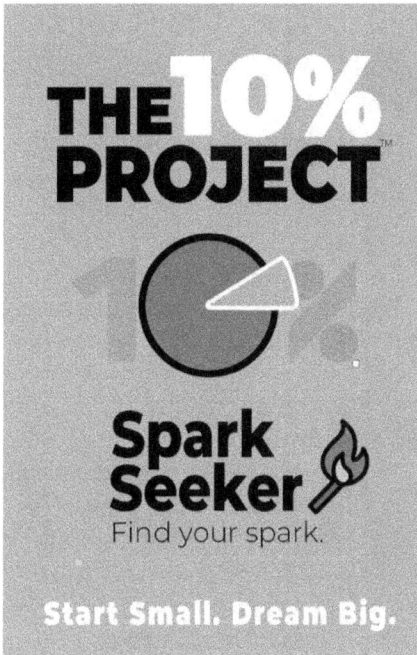

The 10% Project Spark Seeker Reflection Guide

What if the spark for your next small step — toward a life with more meaning, purpose, and joy — is already there... just waiting to be noticed?

The Spark Seeker is your personal reflection guide to help you spot patterns, energy shifts, and everyday inspiration that could lead to your next 10% Project — it is a way to unlock new opportunities to build clarity, confidence, and forward momentum — in your life and work.

Whether you're feeling lit up, burned out, or somewhere in between, this reflection guide helps identify your next small step — with quick, simple prompts to track your energy, spot patterns, and begin building a life powered by what truly sparks you.

- Capture daily highs, lows, and moments of meaning.
- Discover which Spark Zone™ lights you up most — Builder, Solver, Connector, and more.
- Reflect on daily activities, meetings, projects, and experiences with simple prompts and emoji-based mood tracking.
- Translate insights into real momentum with monthly Spark Summaries and 10% Project prompts.

**Because when you know what fuels you...
you can build a life powered by purpose.**

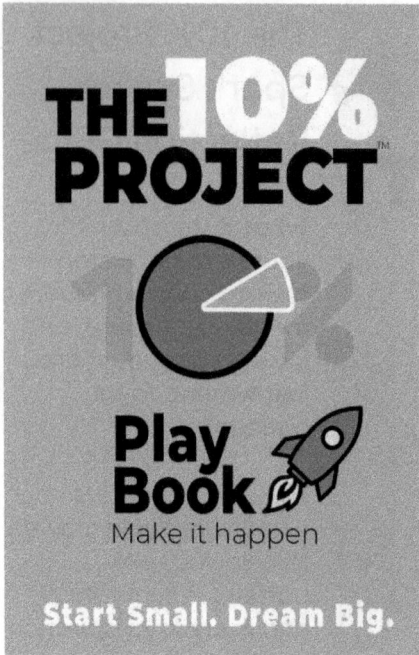

The 10% Project Playbook

What if the spark you've been waiting for... is ready to light a fire?

The 10% Project Playbook is your action companion — designed to help you move from insight to implementation, one small bold step at a time. Whether your project is personal, professional, or still taking shape, this hands-on guide gives you the structure, confidence, and clarity to bring your 10% Project to life.

- Simple frameworks to define and launch your 10% Project.
- Prompts and progress tools to stay focused and motivated.
- Mindset shifts to navigate fear, perfectionism, and "not ready yet".
- Space to reflect, track wins, and build momentum that lasts.
- Motivational reminders to keep you moving forward.

Whether you're bursting with ideas or just beginning to find your spark, this Playbook helps you turn possibility into progress — with purpose at the center.

Because the moment you start, everything changes. And 10% is all you need.

APPENDIX 2

Frequently Asked Questions

Questions That Sparked More Than Answers

This section is dedicated to the incredible people who asked bold, curious, and sometimes wonderfully unexpected questions along the way.

Your curiosity challenged me, your reflections sharpened my thinking, and your "what ifs" turned into whole new chapters.

These aren't just answers—they're conversations in motion. Thank you for pushing this project to be deeper, braver, and more real.

QUESTION:

What's the Difference Between a 10% Project and a Hobby?

ANSWER:

At first glance, a hobby and a 10% Project can look pretty similar. Both involve doing something you enjoy. Both can light you up, challenge you, and even reduce stress.

But here's the key difference:

A hobby is something you do *purely* for enjoyment.

- It's about relaxing, recharging, or simply passing time doing something you love.
- The act of doing the hobby is the goal itself — there's no bigger plan involved.

A 10% Project is more *strategic.*

- It's still built around something that excites you — but it's *intentional* and *tangible.*
- You're carving out 10% of your time to focus on a project that stretches you in a meaningful way:
  - Building new skills.
  - Gaining new experiences.
  - Expanding your network.

Closing a gap or moving toward an opportunity.

You usually have a direction or goal in mind — even if you're not sure exactly where it'll lead yet.

The spark behind a 10% Project comes from curiosity, growth, and strategy — not just passing time.

It's about exploring an area that could unlock doors, create momentum, and open possibilities you might not even see yet.

You don't have to know exactly what the outcome will be. You just need to be *intentional* about why you're doing it — and trust that even small steps can build toward something amazing.

QUESTION:

What do you do if no one believes in your 10% Project?

ANSWER:

You believe in it anyway.

You start small.
You protect the spark.
You work on it in the quiet until it starts to shine — and then, **they notice.**

Some of the best 10% Projects don't start with applause —
they start with raised eyebrows, awkward silences, or people
saying:

"Interesting, are you really doing that?"

And you know what?
You do it anyway.

Because the point isn't to prove something to *them*.
The point is to build something for *you.*

And once you do — once there's motion, once there's joy,
once there's **progress** — then you'll discover people will start
to view it differently.

QUESTION:

What to do when people say no?

ANSWER:

First — hear it.
Then — think.

"No" doesn't mean your idea is wrong.
It just means they don't see what you see... *yet.*

Sometimes people say no because:

- They're too busy.
- They don't get it yet.
- They're afraid of change.
- They're protecting something else that matters to
  them.

That's human.

But your job isn't to argue, or push, or change their minds.
Your job is to keep moving — thoughtfully.

"No" isn't a wall.
It's a redirection sign.

- Try another route.
- Try another person.
- Try another version of your project.

And sometimes, the best move is to tuck your original idea into your 10% Project file, save it for another day, and shift your focus to something else that's ready now.

No idea is ever wasted.
Sometimes it's just waiting for the right time.

Every "yes" you eventually get will feel 10x better because of the "no" that came before it.

"No" is a step. Not a stop.

QUESTION:

What's the link between mentoring and a 10% Project?

ANSWER:

A 10% Project is *your spark.*
Mentoring is *your accelerant.*

Mentors help you:

- See yourself more clearly.
- Stretch into bolder spaces.
- Stay accountable when you want to quit.

- Spot shortcuts you didn't know existed.

And the best part?

A 10% Project gives mentors something real to respond to.

Instead of vague advice like *"just network more"* — you can say: *"Hey, I'm working on a 10% Project — I'd love your insight."*

Now they're not just mentoring your *potential.*
They're mentoring your *momentum.*

Mentoring makes your 10% Project stronger.
And your 10% Project makes mentoring *real.*

Spark + Support = Serious Growth.

QUESTION:

Why did you choose 10% of your time?

ANSWER:

Because 10% is **just enough to matter** —
without being so big that it breaks everything else.

It's enough to:

- Build momentum.
- Try new ideas.
- Create progress you can feel.

And still keep your day job running:

- You don't need to quit.
- You don't need a sabbatical.

◐ You just need **10%** of your time and courage.

More than that? Sure — some people grow their 10% Project into a 15%, 20%, even 40% over time, and sometimes it becomes their new full-time job.

But 10% is the entry point.

It's the *proof of concept* that even a little effort, focused in the right direction, can spark something life changing.

It's small by design — because most of us need to start before we feel ready.

QUESTION:

What is the difference between a Work 10% Project and a Home 10% Project?

ANSWER:

A **Work 10% Project** is about *professional momentum.*
It's something you do **within** or **around** your job that helps you grow, stretch, or lead in new ways.

Examples could include:

◐ Launching a new onboarding guide.

◐ Mentoring a junior teammate.

◐ Starting a workplace storytelling series.

◐ Prototyping an internal tool or training.

◐ Organizing a lunchtime speaker event.

These projects build visibility, skill, and confidence at work — without needing a promotion to do it.

A **Home 10% Project** is about *personal growth, curiosity, or joy.*

It's something outside your job that re-energizes you — but often spills back *into* your work in powerful ways.

Examples could include:

- Starting a podcast.
- Learning to paint.
- Volunteering with teens.
- Writing a play.
- Building a community garden.
- Launching a small business experiment.
- Writing a book.

Sometimes a Home 10% Project even *becomes* your next Work opportunity.

A 10% Project at work helps you move forward at work. A 10% Project at home helps you come alive — and that matters just as much.

QUESTION:

Can you do a personal 10% Project at work?

ANSWER:

It depends — but sometimes that's where the magic happens. A personal 10% Project doesn't have to feel like traditional "work" to belong in the workplace.

But if you're spending 10% of company time on it, your project should generally create **value for your employer.**

That is a good guide to use to determine if your 10% Project is really a work project or a home project. For example, my personal 10% Project – this book – wasn't related to my job,

324 | THE 10% PROJECT

so this was a home 10% Project. I didn't do any of it during working hours.

That said, a work 10% Project doesn't have to be directly tied to your current role. In fact, the more you stretch into new skills, new experiences, and new networks, the better.

But it should still offer something meaningful back to the organization.

Examples might include:

- Starting a gratitude wall or internal newsletter.
- Organizing walking meetings to build community.
- Hosting a team lunch series to practice public speaking.
- Creating a guide to support new hires — because you remember how overwhelming it felt.

It's personal because it matters to *you.*
It's powerful because it often uplifts *everyone else*, too.

And the best part? Sometimes a "personal" project becomes your professional superpower.

Your job is what you're paid to do.
Your 10% Project is what you're called to bring.
And the two can absolutely overlap.

QUESTION:

Why all the Kangaroos?

ANSWER:

Because they carry their spark with them.
Because kangaroos don't walk backwards.
Because they move forward in hops —
just like we do when we're building something brave.

And really...

- They're fun.
- They're weird.
- They're iconic.
- And they totally match the vibe of trying something small and bold — even if you feel a little ridiculous doing it.

The kangaroo is our mascot because it **reminds us to leap** — not perfectly, not with all the answers — but *bravely.*

Just one small bounce at a time.

One hop is enough.
You don't need a runway —
just a pouch full of courage
and a slightly ridiculous grin.

P.S. The fact that I am Australian and my nickname is 'Roo', is just a happy coincidence. ☺

Glossary

Definitions of Key 10% Project Concepts, Sparks, and Psychological Terms

10% Hops™

Tiny, quick, momentum-building micro-actions that activate your spark and move a 10% Project forward. Hops are simple 5–15 minute actions that build clarity and confidence. They come *before* and *within* the Seven 10% Steps™ and represent the smallest unit of progress in the 10% Project.

10% Mindset

A shift from waiting for ideal conditions to starting with what you have. The belief that small, consistent actions create meaningful transformation.

10% Playbook™

A practical, action-oriented guide to the 10% Project — bringing together the Seven 10% Steps™, 10% Hops™, Spark tools, and supporting frameworks into one easy-to-use reference. The 10% Playbook™ distills the core ideas, exercises, checklists, and prompts that help readers turn their spark into meaningful progress. Often used in workshops, coaching, and self-guided 10% Project journeys.

10% Project™

A small, intentional project you devote roughly 10% of your week to. Designed to spark creativity, identity growth, and momentum through consistent, self-directed actions.

10% Theory™

The psychological foundation of the 10% Project: the idea that small, autonomy-driven actions (Hops) support basic psychological needs — autonomy, competence, and relatedness — and gradually lead toward self-actualization and self-transcendence.

Autonomy

The feeling of choice and self-direction. In the 10% Project, autonomy appears when you choose your spark, define your project, design your 'hops', and shape your own path.

Autonomy Support

Creating conditions where people feel free to choose, explore, and express themselves. A key principle in mentoring, leadership, and 10% coaching.

Basic Psychological Needs

The three universal human needs defined in Self-Determination Theory: **autonomy**, **competence**, and **relatedness** — essential for motivation, wellbeing, and growth.

Competence

The feeling of "I can do this." Built through taking small Hops that create skill, confidence, and momentum.

Courage Waves™

Short bursts of bravery that allow you to take a small, meaningful Hop or action. Unpredictable but powerful, these moments often trigger forward movement.

Hop → Step → Jump™

A simple way to understand the rhythm of the 10% Project:

Hop = tiny micro-actions (10% Hops™) that awaken momentum.

Step = the Seven 10% Steps™, the structured framework that organizes your project.

Jump = Step 7 ("Jump Into Action"), the courage moment where planning becomes real movement. Together, these three elements capture how you progress from spark to meaningful change.

Identity Growth

The gradual expansion of how you see yourself through repeated small actions. A 10% Project often transforms identity before it transforms results.

Intrinsic Motivation

Doing something because it is meaningful or interesting to YOU — not for external pressure or reward. The heart of every true 10% Project.

Maslow's Hierarchy of Needs

A human motivation model (1940s–1960s) describing five core needs: physiological, safety, belonging, esteem, and self-actualization — later expanded to include self-transcendence. The 10% Project primarily activates the self-actualization tier.

Micro Activations™

Tiny intentional actions that awaken energy and help you begin. Micro Activations are the cognitive foundation behind **10% Hops™**.

Micro-Bravery

Small acts of courage — sending an email, speaking up, sharing an idea — that help you overcome fear and move forward.

Motivation Loops

A reinforcing cycle where action → energy → more action. The 10% Project harnesses these loops through small Hops.

Relatedness

The feeling of connection, belonging, and support. Often created through mentors, collaborators, friends, and Spark Pods™ connected to your 10% Project.

Roo Room™

A supportive workshop-style environment where people gather to explore sparks, reflect, share wins, and support one another's 10% Projects.

Self-Actualization

Maslow's term for becoming the fullest expression of yourself. The 10% Project is a modern, accessible path into everyday self-actualization through small steps.

Self-Activation™

The process of awakening internal motivation through small, self-chosen actions — the heartbeat of the 10% Project.

Self-Determination Theory (SDT)

A leading motivation theory developed by Edward Deci & Richard Ryan (1970s–1990s). It states that people thrive when autonomy, competence, and relatedness are supported. A core foundation of 10% Theory™.

Self-Transcendence

Maslow's expanded "sixth level" of human motivation — the desire to uplift others and contribute to something bigger. Many 10% Projects naturally evolve here.

Spark™

Your inner pull — an idea, curiosity, or desire that lights you up from the inside. Sparks are the starting point for a 10% Project.

Spark Deck™

A card-based discovery tool used to identify interests, values, and drivers — often used to ignite a spark or find a project.

Spark Pods™

Small, supportive groups (virtual or in-person) where participants share progress, celebrate wins, reflect, and support each other's 10% Projects.

Spark Seeker™

A guided workbook that helps you explore your interests, values, patterns, and ideas — often used before choosing a 10% Project.

Spark Statements™

Short, powerfully clear statements describing what excites or energizes you. Used to guide project selection and stay anchored to your spark.

Spark Zone™

The intersection of what excites you, energizes you, and matters to you. The sweet spot where the best 10% Project ideas live.

The 10% Project 7 Step Framework™

The official, seven-part framework of the 10% Project — a structured path from spark to movement. Not to be confused with **10% Hops™**, which are micro-actions.

Step 1: Ignite Your Spark
Reflect on what matters most right now.

Step 2: Find Your 10% Project
Identify a meaningful idea you can improve, create, or launch.

Step 3: Own It
Define your project clearly. Capture the what, why, and how. Give it a name.

Step 4: Chart the Course
Break your project into small, doable pieces that build momentum.

Step 5: Share the Vision
Tell someone. Invite encouragement, support, or accountability.

Step 6: Reflect and Refine
Review your progress, gather insights, and adjust.

Step 7: Jump Into Action
Take meaningful action — start small, but start.

Acknowledgements & Heartfelt Thanks

This book was born from late-night scribbles, early-morning sparks, long car rides, waiting at ballet lessons, weekends in Tahoe, and an incredible circle of support.

Tom — my gorgeous husband. Thank you for your steady presence, your quiet encouragement, and your uncanny ability to know exactly what I need at exactly the right time (*most* of the time ☺). I couldn't have done this without you. You really are the best husband ever.

Gabby — your creativity, resilience, and giant heart remind me every day why bold steps matter. I love you.

Michael — thank you for your encouragement, your enthusiasm for all things marketing and strategy, and your embrace of so many 10% Projects over the years.

Ace — the powerhouse of cheerleading that kept me awake and moving forward on endless late nights with your endless ideas, enthusiasm, and unwavering support.

To the amazing leaders and students associated with **The Ohio State University**, who first invited me to speak to the MBA students, especially **Dan Oglevee**, **Rob Mullins**, the incredible **Ken Coleman**, **Joe Goodman** who first introduced me to the Self-determination Theory, and of course **Liz Varga** — the student who inspired this crazy idea with her enthusiasm for the earliest concepts of the 10% Project.

To **Tracy Bleile** — who gave me the reason to finally get it done.

To so many incredible managers and leaders who believed in me and encouraged me to do more than I ever imagined — including, but certainly not limited to:

- My early mentors who helped shape my path: **Rosemary Pollock, John Robins, Lenora Brooks, Paul Gargett,** and **Stephen Gumley.**

- Leaders at **The Boeing Company: Dawn Thoresness, John Hayhurst, Beth Kluba, Turbo Sjogren, Rick Stephens, Dennis Muilenburg, Maureen Cragin, Warren Brown, Egan Greenstein, Logan Jones, Steve Nordlund,** and **Dan Korte.**

- The startup champions who gave me the opportunity to grow: **Sebastien de Halleux, Surya Ganti,** and **Seshu Madhavapeddy.**

To all my family, friends, and co-workers who have endured my cunning plans and cheered on my countless crazy ideas — thank you for always being in my corner.

To my early readers, cheerleaders, and co-dreamers — thank you for believing in this project before it even had a name. You helped bring it to life.

To my lifelong friends —**Jeannine Mason, Jeanette Davis,** and **Kim Forkan** — thank you for being there through thick and thin.

To the many others who've supported me in quiet, powerful ways — there are too many to name, but I hope you know who you are... including Jo, Jenn, Joan, Karen (KDD), Aleah, Chelle, David, the list is long...

And to every reader holding this book right now — thank you. May your own 10% Project open new doors you didn't even know were waiting.

www.ingramcontent.com/pod-product-compliance
Lightning Source LLC
Chambersburg PA
CBHW070017100426
42740CB00013B/2537